The **Laureate for Irish Fiction** is an initiative of the Arts Council established to honour an extraordinary Irish writer of prose fiction. Through the public programme, the Laureate for Irish Fiction seeks to encourage a new generation of writers and promote engagement with Irish fiction at home and abroad.

Anne Enright is an internationally acclaimed Irish novelist, essayist and writer of short stories whose work has earned many awards, including the Man Booker Prize (2007) and the Irish Book of the Year (twice). She was the first Laureate for Irish Fiction (2015–18) and is currently Professor of Creative Writing at UCD.

NO
AUTHORITY

NO
AUTHORITY

WRITINGS
FROM THE
LAUREATESHIP

BY
ANNE ENRIGHT

First published 2019
by University College Dublin Press
UCD Humanities Institute,
Room H103
Belfield,
Dublin 4
www.ucdpress.ie

ISBN 978-1-910820-51-3

CIP data available from the British Library

The right of Anne Enright to be identified as the
author of this work has been asserted by her

Design: Daniel Morehead

Printed in England on acid-free paper by
Antony Rowe, Chippenham, Wiltshire

CONTENTS

Introduction | No Authority   1

Lecture 1 | Antigone in Galway   7

Short Story | The Hotel   31

Lecture 2 | Maeve Brennan: Going Mad in New York   41

Short Story | Solstice   59

Lecture 3 | Call yourself George: 69
Gender Representation in the Irish Literary Landscape

Oh Canada: Lecture delivered on the presentation   89
of the UCD Ulysses Medal to Margaret Atwood

Afterword | Ennis, Armagh, Howth and Ballymun: 101
A Report from the Laureate 2015–18

Trump's victory in November 2016 was preceded, in my home life, by the death of my father in early June. I had lost a wonderful man from my life while the world gained a terrible one, and for many months I found it hard to look up to anyone who claimed to be in charge of anything, especially if they were male.

My father was a quiet man, gentle and smart, and an astute observer of his children. He could fix sleeplessness and toothache, he took temperatures, checked for appendicitis. There was no bombast or posturing. He was one of those Irish countrymen who is amazed by their daughters: the fact of their femaleness was an added wonder in his day. I am trying to find something negative to say about the man – he smoked non-stop and absented himself sometimes in deafness, but he was, by the world's standards as well as by my own, a very good person; extremely slow to anger, a punner and puzzler, a lover of languages, with great independence of mind. His children took his advice because it came so rarely. He did not follow the crowd. Donal Enright was from County Clare: he never seemed to break any rules, and he never once did what he was told.

Five months later, my thoughts were full of Trump, who seemed to be the opposite of my father in all the important ways. And although the man was nothing to me, I was not the only person on the planet to take his election personally. Hundreds of thousands of women took to the streets in cities all over the world to raise their voices against this man, and what he stood for, and we marched again, in Dublin, for the pro-choice campaign to repeal the 8th amendment. Trump made the problem for women clear. Trump *was* the problem. The question was, who had put the problem itself in charge of America?

His voters polled strongly for 'authoritarianism', we were told – a psychologist's term used to describe people who seek strong men and hold the weak in disdain. They like to follow the rules, valuing obedience and respect for authority 'no matter what'.

It is too easy to say facile things about voters, but it became quickly apparent that 'No matter what', could be the man's motto. It would be a mistake to call the man an authority in the usual sense. The confusion of his first months came, in part, from liberals who wanted a properly Presidential figure, and could not understand that they had got something else, now. This is a man who does not do what he is told, or so he would have us think: at his rallies he complains non-stop about the serious turn his life has taken. As authorities go, Trump is pretty much a child. It took a while to see that his childishness was a distraction from more sinister content: an unsayable understanding about whiteness, maleness, dominance and greed. Trump is, or pretends to be, infantile. He has been described as 're-infantilising the masses' in the term used by Freud to describe the rise of Fascism in the 1930s. His personal dysfunction has become embodied and magnified by the crowd.

The death of my father in June already left me feeling exposed to misogynies, hidden and overt. After he died, I felt the world's unfairness. I am not sure why. Perhaps, when he was alive I had recourse to a figure who was, in my head, more important than any other man. Some childlike part of me needed this and mourned it. I needed to be told I was valued – and in order for those words to have weight, I needed them to come from on high.

If I was a child while my father still lived, in November I fell into an astonished and rancorous middle age. The men out in the world are not your father, that is for sure. Men still organise their hierarchies of value in a way that excludes women, at least they do if we let them. It seems to be some kind of default. I wondered if the exclusion of women was not axiomatic to the sense of male importance – as it used to be when they were eight years old. Some unsayable truth had been lurking under the illusion of change, and now it was out in the open. Misogyny, I thought, ruled the world.

My tolerance for the misogynists I know, in all their unhappiness, evaporated. The #metoo movement helped: it was as if some magnetic bond between women and men's badness had suddenly stopped working. And though it was good to stand free of that, the debate about sex and sexual predation left other questions unanswered. Because, when I thought about it, I knew many good men and very few bad ones. Was this male goodness also illusory? What, I wondered, came between these individual, well intentioned men and the wider enactment of equality?

Once you saw the pictures of Trump's first cabinet, every other group photograph became gendered in a similar way: open the paper to see a bunch of powerful and important Irish men, followed by another bunch of Irish men, some of them people you know. And because these men were not willing to talk about how good or bad it felt to be in that photograph, it was up to the viewer to consider the connection between individual men and institutional power.

I also wondered why it was, that, for a woman, being in the company of one or two men can be a good way to pass the time and being in a room with ten men hard to enjoy. I am not talking about rugby teams here, although these can be terrifying to women, especially after dark. I am talking about the ten men who run your company, the ten men on the county council or at the editorial meeting, the undifferentiated, often besuited maleness that struggles to include women, for reasons they do not want to articulate.

When I looked at my own business of writing books, where unfairness is hard to identify, I found a reluctance among men to read or review books by women and it was hard not to see an aversion to the feminine there. The game of literary reputation is also a game about authority. Who writes the important story? Who says it is important? Both these questions were questions about being in charge.

I have never been good with authority. If I had a more compliant personality, I would have lived a less creative life, I think, though I was getting tired, in middle age, of dodging something, in my head. I started to ask myself, who I was trying to annoy – isn't this just the same as trying to please them? What was important about being important, after all?

Meanwhile, my own anger was worth considering. After my father died, there was no big man who was above it all – above the business of gender or misogyny, above the grubby business of competition and dominance – there was no one who could keep things fair.

And I missed that. I mourned the loss, not just of my father, but also of some ideal man, the right-thinking judge, the ultimate authority. In order to compass my hurt, I had to acknowledge my need for a superior goodness in the world. I also had to question why, even though I was a woman and a feminist, my idea of authority – in some lovely, secret way – tilted male. Or it skewed male in some terrible, exclusionary way. Perhaps these contradictory feelings were both aspects of the same childlike need.

The danger with something that is not real – as my idealised sense of my father's authority is not quite real – is that it can turn very simply into its opposite. The rise of Trump was a terrific reminder that there is enough childishness in the world already. It was time to grow up. It was also time to be the figure I needed in my life, to work on a horizontal axis, look at things straight. It was time to judge things, not as I wanted them to be, but as they were. It was time I stopped looking upwards, for the big man who wasn't there.

When I was appointed as Laureate of Irish Fiction in 2015, I also had no idea how to step up into the role. Two of these pieces are short stories written for an annual curated event: The Long Night of the Short Story, which took place on 21st December, each year of my tenure, in Galway, Dublin and Carlow. There is also a report on the current state of Irish writing in translation which was published by the *Irish Times*. The most challenging part of the job was the invitation to write an annual lecture. This I accepted with some seriousness, not realising that the thoughts I was trying to articulate on a personal level would be part of a general chorus about women's voices in the world. Who knew, in 2015, what lay ahead of us? These writings are my blundering attempt to find clarity, in a confusing time.

ANTIGONE IN GALWAY

'IT WAS THE LITTLE ONES THEMSELVES CRYING OUT TO ME'

In September, the Irish government held a state funeral for the exhumed remains of Thomas Kent, a rebel and patriot, who was executed in 1916 and buried in the yard of what is now Cork Prison. The prison is at the rear of Collins Barracks, once the Victoria Barracks, and Kent's coffin was first removed to the Garrison church where thousands of people – including Dr John Buckley, the Bishop of Cork and Ross – filed past to pay their respects. The funeral echoed the reinternment of Roger Casement – thrown in a lime pit in Pentonville Prison in 1916 and repatriated in 1965 – when Éamon de Valera got out of his sickbed to attend and a million people lined the route. Thomas Kent was buried in the family plot at Castlelyons and the Taoiseach, Enda Kenny, gave the graveside oration. 'Today,' he said, 'We take him from the political Potter's Field to lay him with all honour among 'his own'.' Although the land in which he had lain is now, technically speaking, Irish, the prison yard still held the taint of Britishness or the memory of his dishonour.

'Potter's Field' is not a term much used in Ireland, though we have many traditional burial plots for strangers. These are marked 'Cillíní' on the Ordnance Survey maps. Sometimes translated as 'children's graveyard', the sites contain the graves of unbaptised infants, but also of women who died in childbirth, 'changeling' children, suicides, executed criminals and the insane (infanticides were typically disposed of without burial). Some are situated on sacred sites and in ancestral burial grounds that existed before the shift that happened, in early medieval Ireland, to the churchyard. These earlier graves served a territorial function: they are found near the boundaries of ancient kingdoms, and by the water's edge. Cillíní are often situated between one place and another, at the limits of things. After the Second Vatican Council abolished limbo in the early 60s, they fell out of use.

Some of those I visited in Connemara command a mighty view. One lies beside a path known as Mámean (the pass of the birds) that pilgrims still use on the way to the well of St Patrick. Individual graves are built up with large stones, for the length of the body beneath, and there are no crosses to be seen. The bodies of infants were buried by a father or an uncle, often at night. The scant ritual and the isolation of the setting is offset by the beauty that surrounds it: the place feels both abandoned and sacred. Which is not to say that the women whose babies were so buried did not resent the lack of a marker or feel the loneliness of the spot (if they were told, indeed, where it was). It was a great difficulty to have someone close to you, buried apart. Irish graveyards are, above all, family places. 'Would you like to be buried with my people?' is not a marriage proposal you might hear in another country, not even as a joke.

Emigration split families, and this may have made the need to gather together stronger for those who remained, even after death. In a country of the dispossessed, it is also tempting to see the grave plot as a treasured piece of land. But the drama of the Irish graveyard was not about ownership, and only partly about honour (in the Traveller community, to step on a grave is still an indelible insult). Irish ghost stories tell of graveyards actually rejecting those who do not belong – by which is meant, Protestants. The ground itself might refuse, and yield their bodies up, or if they did stay put, the wall could jump over them in the night, to put the Protestant on the other side. Whole churchyards went wandering in order to leave them behind. I am sure these ideas of purity and aversion apply to more than the Irish dead but they persist well enough in modern times to make Antigone a less than notional experience about the symbolic and political order. It is not just about the mourning female voice, or about kinship and the law, it is also a play about the political meaning of the body, after death.

When Enda Kenny praised the nieces, who lobbied for the reinternment of Thomas Kent: 'These three women have tended the flame of his memory', he was speaking from the heart of the Irish rhetorical tradition. Under the censorship of British rule, the graveside was a rare opportunity for political speech, and it was a woman's role not just to mourn and love, but also to remember the revolutionary martyr. The job of remembering was also a work of silence; 'Who dares to speak of '98' says J. K. Ingram in *The Memory of the Dead*, a poem which commemorates the rebellion of 1798 'Silent oh Moyle be the roar of the waters' was the song by Thomas Moore, who also wrote: 'Oh breathe not his name!' The name being that of executed patriot Robert Emmet who asked his epitaph remain unwritten until his country had taken its place among the nations of the earth. High speech and silence, this was the patriotic way, and no silence more urgent than that of the graveyard. And so we get the great speech by Pearse, eight months before the 1916 Rising: 'the fools, the fools, the fools! – they have left us our Fenian dead, and while Ireland holds these graves, Ireland unfree shall never be at peace.'

Creon, the ruler of the city, dishonours the body of his nephew to serve as a warning to other potential enemies of the state. One brother, Eteocles, has been buried 'in accordance with justice and law', the other Polyneices 'is to lie unwept and unburied': this according to their sister Antigone, who has already, at the play's opening, decided to ignore Creon's edict and bury the corpse. And so she does. When asked to deny the crime, she says, 'I did the deed I do not deny it.' She does not seek to justify her actions within the terms of Creon's law: she negates the law by handing it back to him, intact. 'If you call that law', she says.

Antigone, in the translation by Anne Carson, later says she is being punished for 'an act of perfect piety', but that act is also in the play, perfectly wordless. The speeches she makes to her sister Ismene and to Creon are before and after the fact. She is a woman who breaks an unjust law. We can ask if she does this from inside or outside the legal or linguistic system of the play, or of the state, but it is good to bear in mind that Antigone does not bury her brother with words, but with dust.

Her appeal when she makes it, is, not to Creon but to a higher order of justice; 'the unwritten unfaltering unshakeable ordinances of the gods.' Antigone looks into her heart, you might think, and towards the heavens, while Creon looks around him to the business of government. But this system collapses, before the end of the play, into something more simple and self-enclosed. 'The dead do not belong to you,' Tiresias tells Creon, 'nor to the gods above.' There are moments – and death (or more properly decay) is one of them – that belong to neither sacred nor secular law, but to themselves. Antigone has known this all along: 'Death needs to have Death's laws obeyed.'

Carson's doesn't use the word, 'ghost'. The idea that Polyneices has some residual agency or voice creeps into other translations, but not into this one. The body remains a body – rawflesh for dogs and birds – not a human presence. It is only when Antigone herself goes to die that she calls her brother's name.

'They say a grave never settles,' Catherine Corless says to me as we walk the convent wall, in Tuam, where she suspects adult remains may lie. I look at the ground and I can believe it, the shadow of vegetation that grows more lush, in an oblong, six feet by four. This is beyond the little plot where locals say that babies from the local Mother and Baby Home were buried. There is a small grotto in the corner, tended by the residents of the housing estate that was built on the site in the early 70s. Corless was doing a local history project on the place and, intrigued by the unmarked burial plot, went to the Bon Secours Sisters to ask for records. These had been been passed on to the County Council in Galway, they said. The County Council told her they were passed on to the Health Board, the Health Board said they had only 'individual records' which she would not be allowed to see. She then went to the Births, Marriages and Deaths Registration Office in Galway to get, at her own expense, the death certificates of 796 babies and children who died in the Mother and Baby Home in Tuam, between 1925 and 1961. The location of their bodies is unrecorded, they have not yet been found.

There was a local story told of boys who had, in 1975, seen the small bones of children in some kind of tank, under a broken concrete top. There was a strong response from the media when Corless said that this might be a disused septic tank that is marked on the map as lying under this spot. There was much rifling through the statistics and records – yes, the death rate among illegitimate children was up to five times that of those born within marriage, but institutions are great places for disease to spread, and what about measles? In fact, Corless was accusing no one of murder, and besides, the story was not new. There had been a brief report in a local paper two years previously, and no one had seemed to care. It was the word 'septic' that did it; the association with sewage, the implication that the bodies were not just carelessly buried, or even discarded, but treated like 'filth' itself. After the words 'septic tank' appeared in the world's press Corless found herself besieged by journalists. She was misquoted, then called a liar for things she had not said. With all that shame flying around, it needed a place to stick. And clearly it was her fault, whatever it was: the sewage tanks, the babies, all that dead history – Ireland's reputation abroad.

Catherine Corless is a steady, unassuming person, with great focus. She lives in a well-tended farmhouse, at the centre of a loyal family, and does not mix much with the wider world. The kitchen table, when I visit, is covered with maps, photocopies, ledgers, certificates. As I talk to her, two people ring her mobile phone – they are looking for female relatives who may have been in the Tuam Mother and Baby Home.

They may already have asked the nuns and the County Council and the Health Board, but even adoptees born in the home do not have the statutory right to see their records, this is because of the secrecy clauses signed by the mothers who, willingly or not, gave them away. The information they do find may have been falsified at the time and people are maddened by all this. I mean, they are driven pure mad. So, there is great desperation in the searches that lead people to local historians like Corless, who is not paid for the work she does on their behalf. She tells me about a man she helped, who was born in the home, of an unmarried mother. The man was 70. He had led a full life. He had six children of his own, but one of them was disabled and he thought this was a punishment of some kind. When he found his mother's grave, he brought flowers to it, and wept. He just wanted to meet her, he said, and tell her that it was all right.

Corless seems a pragmatic person, but she has a quietly passionate turn of phrase. When I ask her why she brought the problem of the missing dead to light, she says, 'It was the little ones themselves crying out to me.'

Her interest in historical research began when, after the death of her own mother, she tried to trace her origins. There was 'some load there, some secret'. Catherine's grandmother entered a second relationship with a Protestant man, her mother was fostered out and she never went back home. Corless managed to trace an aunt and when she made contact, decades after these events, the woman said, 'We have nothing here for you now.'

Her mother was always belittling herself, Corless says. 'She took hurt into her, but she never hurt anyone.' It is the same with women she has met who were the victims of Catholic institutional care: 'these people are as gentle and as nice.' As I am talking to Catherine, the thing I find suddenly striking is how few nuns it took to run the Mother and Baby Home – four or five, she says, for up to a hundred pregnant and nursing women, and their children, who might be taken away for adoption at any time. They sound so compliant. What were they like?

Fear, says Corless, the threat of being sent to the asylum or the laundry, that according to Julia, a long-term resident: 'is how the argument is settled.'

Dr Coughlan was GP for the Galway Magdalene Laundry from 1981 to 1984. He says,

The Residents were a delightful and happy group of ladies ... each lady presented as a unique individual, with a unique personality, well able to ask relevant questions and to express her opinion and, above all, ready and willing to gossip, to tease and be teased and to joke.

Perhaps it is true. Irish women are often nice.

When the Bon Secours Nuns left Tuam for good they exhumed the remains of their dead sisters – twelve in all – and took them with them to their new home in Knock. The controversy Corless started about the 796 missing bodies has provoked a new commission of enquiry, this time into the Mother and Baby Homes in Ireland, led by Judge Yvonne Murphy. A few weeks ago, an archeological survey was taken of the ground using ground penetrating radar and magnetometry. Corless welcomed the move, confident that the remains of an untold number of children will be found there. But if they are not found – and that is also possible – then she will be again to blame, and there will be much fuss and distraction from the fact that no one knows where the 796 bodies have gone.

The living can be disbelieved, dismissed, but the dead do not lie. We turn, in death, from witness to evidence, and this evidence is indelible, because it is mute.

It all started in 1993, when the Sisters of Our Lady of Charity of Refuge sold off a portion of their land to a developer in order to cover recent losses on the stock exchange. As part of the deal, they exhumed a mass grave on the site which contained the bodies of Auxiliaries – women who worked until their deaths in the Magdalene Laundry of High Park – which closed in 1991.

There were ten of these laundries in Ireland. They are styled, by the nuns who ran them, as refuges for marginalised women, where they endured, along with their keepers, an enclosed, monastic life of work and prayer. The women were described as 'penitents', and the act of washing was seen as symbolic. The laundries were run as active concerns, washing the dirty linen for hotels, hospitals and the army, and they undercut their rivals in the trade by the fact that their penitential workforce was not paid. So, the laundries might also be styled as labour camps, or prison camps, where women were sent, without trial, for a crime that was hard to name. In 1958, 70 per cent of the women in the Magdalene Laundry in Galway were unmarried mothers. Asked how long they would be there, the Mother Superior answered, 'Some stay for life.'

To the apparent surprise of the Sisters of Our Lady of Charity of Refuge 22 extra bodies were found in the opened grave at High Park. The nuns did not appear to know the names of several of the women, listing them by their religious names as Magdalene of St Cecilia, Magdalene of Lourdes, and over one third of the 155 deaths had never been certified. It was clear the nuns were not used to dealing with outside authorities. Costs were high; they allegedly haggled with the undertaker to ask if they could get three bodies per coffin. In the end, the remains were cremated, in contravention of Catholic custom, and everyone who heard the news then or read the reports knew, in the silence of their hearts, exactly what was going on, and what had been going on, and what all this meant.

It was another ten years before journalist Mary Raftery wrote about the High Park exhumations. Raftery's documentaries, the three part, *States of Fear* (1999) and *Cardinal Secrets* (2002) provoked two commissions of enquiry, one into abuse in Irish institutions for children, which were usually run by the religious, and one into clerical abuse in the Dublin Archdiocese. These were published in 2009 as the Ryan Report and the Murphy Report, respectively. Before her death in 2012, she was hailed as the most influential broadcaster of her day, but Raftery got what we used to call 'drag' from RTE television on these projects, especially *States of Fear*; the kind of delay, indifference and non-compliance that runs through an institution when someone seeks to disturb the status quo. Sheila Ahern, who worked with her as a lone researcher, remembers being told that the story was, in media terms, 'done already'. There was no budget, no resources, the whole thing was deemed, in audience terms, 'a turn off', and Raftery was asked to 'lighten it up a bit', for being too grim. Mostly patronising, this is an attitude that only turns aggressive at the last moment; it is particularly suited to dealing with women when they are troublesome, and Mary Raftery was very troublesome. Passionate for the victims of abuse, she had a bad attitude when it came to authority: non-compliant, endlessly tenacious, and full of glee.

I don't think a man could have done what she did, but it would be wrong to cast Raftery as some kind of Antigone: all her concern was for the living. Her work was founded on personal testimony of people who had been abused in institutions. Some of these people may have spoken on the radio in the late 90s, but she brought those voices into vision, and shaped an argument with and around them that was incontrovertible. These people had been, for some reason, hard to hear, now you could not look away – their stories were unbearable, and for the country, deeply shaming. Bertie Aherne, the then Taoiseach, issued an apology before the third part of the series hit air.

Raftery worked within the law, sharing the churches and the state's obsession with records, files, account books, ledgers, baptismal certificates, adoption papers, gravestones and mortal remains. She took an almost child-like pleasure undoing the riddle of power. I knew her a little. She was good fun. One of our conversations was about the redress scheme established in 2002 as a result of her work, to compensate those who had suffered abuse in childcare institutions. This seemed to me like a good thing. But the money, Raftery said, was subject to a confidentiality clause and this recalled, for some victims, the secrecy imposed on them by their abusers, the small bribes they used: a bit of chocolate, a hug. 'You see?' she said. Back in the trap.

In the late 1980s I met a woman who had been committed to St Ita's, a mental institution in North County Dublin. The papers were signed by her mother and a priest. The priest had the power to sign a section order in those days – though a doctor might also have been involved. The priest was the woman's uncle, her mother's brother, and they were putting her away because she said he, the priest, had felt her up. This was a woman my own age, or younger. In St Ita's she was medicated for three months and kept her in for another three, and then they let her go. The doctors knew there was nothing wrong with her, she said. I remember laughing in horror at this story, and she laughed too. 'They have you every way.'

It is, of course, this woman's mother who is the most interesting person in this story; how she disbelieved her daughter and pushed her away. The graveyard at St Ita's is a walled plot that contains, by repute, 5,000 bodies. There is only one personal headstone – raised by an inmate's uncle, on behalf of his grieving sister, in the early 1900s. The priest at Grangegorman, another huge asylum, got so lonely burying the abandoned mad that he requested company from the staff – just one other living person, to say the word, 'Amen.'

The dead, we feel, should be freed from the sorrows of the living. The shame should leave them with their last breath. They should be allowed back in.

'That boy is dead, says Tiresias to Creon 'stop killing him.'

Instead, Creon kills Antigone. He kills his own future daughter-in-law, breaking his son's heart. Creon is concerned with anarchy: 'obedience saves lives'; and by the need to stay superior to womankind 'never never let ourselves be bested by a woman'. He is also concerned with pollution. His son's nature has been 'polluted' by being subject to a woman. The pleasure of sex that women afford is, 'an open wound in your honour and your life.'

Creon is speaking about all women here, but Antigone is like a woman squared, being the product of an incestuous union between her father, Oedipus, and his mother, Jocasta. Their family, says Ismene, is 'doubled tripled degraded and dirty in every direction.' The line of kinship is hopelessly tangled, so when Ismene says, 'Oh sister do not cross this line', she is speaking to someone in whom all boundaries are broken.

The line of Creon's edict is only one of the 'lines' in the play. There is the city wall, and there is also the horizon line, where Polyneices' body lies on the unopening ground.

Antigone neither outside nor inside. She is 'a strange new inbetween thing … not at home with the dead nor with the living.' As the play proceeds she moves deeper into the other world, 'my soul died long ago,' she says, 'so it might serve the dead.' This self-involvement makes her seem a bit adolescent in the face of Creon's unyielding, corporate, fury. She is like a teenager 'doing' death – but this is not a rehearsal of adult autonomy: Antigone is buried alive by way of punishment for her crime. As she goes to her tomb – she calls it 'a bridal chamber' – she looks to her own incestuous contradictions, calling out to 'her people', father, mother and brother.

She is, according to the chorus: 'the only one of mortals to go down to Death alive.' The paradox of living death completes the incestuous paradox of her origins. It is like a bad joke. Antigone is a pun that was never funny. She had nothing to lose.

Creon is, by contrast, free of incestuous taint. 'a man who runs his household right/ can run a government.' To be a man is to be a man. He will not get mixed up in her or by her. In order to stay whole and free he must assert his authority: he must kill Antigone. If he lets her away with it then: 'surely I am not a man here/ she is the man.' He will put some food in her burial chamber, 'just enough to avoid pollution/ a sort of / sacred technicality.' He 'will clean the city of this girl'. When his son kills himself Creon bemoans his own folly and the god who was his undoing, but the sight of his wife's corpse makes him cry: 'Oh filth of death', and he becomes 'utterly blended with pain'. By trying to keep himself clean and separate – from the incestuous, from the female, from death itself – Creon has fallen into a different trap. 'If you find you're confusing evil with good/ some god is heading you down the high road to ruin.' It is Tiresias, history's first transexual, who puts him straight: 'for you've housed a living soul beneath the ground below / and held a dead man here/ without his grave or rights.' Sometimes the things we had said all our lives look strange again, like the way the religious style themselves as family: Father, Mother, Brother, Sister.

It is hard to say if it is a question of aversion, of purity or of privacy, but the nuns plot in High Park was as far as the land would allow from that of the Auxiliaries. This is also true of Sunday's Well Magdalene Laundry in Cork – the nuns are in the northeastern corner, in neat rows with a plain cross for each, the Auxiliaries are in a mass grave, now vandalised, in an overgrown and inaccessible part of the complex. Ordinary Magdalenes were buried in the local public cemetery, though anxiety persists about the names on their headstones and the actual occupants of the graves. This anxiety was not alleviated by the most recent report, in a line of reports: The Inter-Departmental Committee to establish the facts of State Involvement with the Magdalene Laundries (IDC) – known as the McAleese Report – which was published in 2013.

Martin McAleese trained as a dentist and as an accountant and served the state well as the spouse of President Mary McAleese over 14 years, in which time he played an active role in the Northern Irish Peace Process. In his executive summary McAleese says he wants to protect the privacy of the Magdalene workers, who have, for too long, suffered the stigma of being called 'fallen women'. They came to the homes through various routes, the courts, the industrial schools, by free will and at the behest of their families. He stresses that they were not prostitutes, as commonly thought, and hopes this label will not simply be replaced with the word 'criminal'. He does not mention the privacy of the nuns, or their potential 'criminality', these are not at issue. The congregations have since refused either to apologise or to contribute to any redress scheme.

Published in 2013, the Report is a strange document. The first mention that the women were not paid for their work comes in Chapter 15, in a section about social insurance. There is another reference to their lack of wages in Chapter 19. And that's it, really, on the slavery question. The report is 1000 pages long. And money is much discussed. Accounts are provided, to show that the laundries operated on a 'break-even basis'. These were furnished by the congregations to their own accountants and were not subject to separate audit.

Some accounts are listed as missing, including that of Sunday's Well in Cork. One-time RTE researcher Sheila Ahern came into possession of accounts for Sunday's Well dealing with the years from 1957 to 1966. She photocopied them and posted the originals back to the nuns of The Good Shepherd, who, in March 1999 wrote back to Mary Raftery, saying, 'The 43,950 from the laundry was the only funding available for the 130 or so women who essentially had no state funding or support... We would ask that you look at the overall situation in context.' Ofcourse these accounts might have been subsequently lost by the nuns of the Good Shepherd so we cannot say that the IDC was less than obsessive in its hunt for the truth. Still it is an odd - almost journalistic – thrill to look at copies of documents on your own laptop that the public record says do not exist.

Broadly speaking, the report asks us to believe that women working an eight or ten-hour day ('we never knew the time' says one) for six days a week, before falling asleep in unheated dormitories, could not earn enough to keep themselves fed. If the nuns were bad with money, they were like no nuns I ever knew, but the issue of profitability is another distraction. The question is not one of business management, but of human rights. Why do we feel confused?

The advocacy group – Justice for Magdalenes – has challenged the IDC's findings about the number of women in the system and about the average duration of stay. The report puts this at 3.22 years, with a median of 27.6 weeks, but this ignores women who went in before independence in 1922, many of whom stayed for life. Claire McGettrick has checked electoral registers to find that 63.1 per cent of adult women registered in the Donnybrook Magdalen Laundry in 1954–5 were still there nine years later. Local grave records show that over half of the women on electoral registers between 1954 and 1964 died at that institution.

The Magdalene story, like the other stories here, is one of people maddened by information, misinformation, lies and ledgers, and there is much and persuasive talk of statistics. But it is the voices of the women that interest me. They spoke to McAleese in person. The report breaks their testimony into different categories, moving from 'sexual abuse' through 'physical abuse' through to 'lack of information and a real fear of remaining there until death'. Only one woman complains that she was not paid for her work. Perhaps the others did not feel entitled to pay, or entitled, indeed, to complain. Their ideas of difficulty might be different to yours or mine. The report uses their voices in brief quotations to say that there was no sexual abuse, there was very little physical abuse (by which is meant beatings), there was ritual humiliation, long hours of thankless labour, bewilderment and fear.

But you know, it wasn't as bad as you might think. Many, many times longer than any woman's testimony is that offered by Dr Coughlan who seemed to have had a splendid time in the Galway Laundry: 'After I sat down at my desk a jovial Resident would proudly arrive with a linen-covered tray laden with tea and buns.' The ladies wore colourful clothing, they brought him their small troubles, or bits of gossip 'Do you like my hair, Doctor?' There was rarely anything wrong with them, medically, 'Overall, my experience with the Magdalen was a happy and gratifying one.' And as for death certs, he often had to tell people about death certs, we can assume he was worn out telling them.

The women Dr Coughlan saw in 1984 were among the last Magdalenes. It is possible they were institutionalised, though he sees that damage as a kind of sweetness. It is possible – though it is really not possible – that it wasn't all that bad and, besides, it is fine now.

The fragmentation of the women's testimony – they are turned into a kind of chorus by in the report – seems to show some unease. Justice for Magdalenes say that McAleese was at first reluctant to speak to the former inmates at all, also that 'Survivors were not made aware their responses would be used to cast doubt over their abusive experiences.' Ofcourse the report is not an oral history project, nor even a history project, and it fulfilled its remit to prove there was significant state involvement in the laundries, but I felt I knew less after it, somehow, than before. It is hard to describe how tiring it was to work through – chasing the sense that something is missing, that you are trapped within the paternalistic paradox: *I am in charge therefore, you are fine.*

So, the Taoiseach said sorry, and there is now a redress scheme in place. The records, which McAleese said were so willingly opened to him by the congregations have been anonymised and returned.

Times were different, this is what the men in my life say, my father, my brother, my husband. Martin, my husband, says that for the Athenian audience Creon was the hero of the piece; his was the hubris, and his, the fall. Creon tries to control the natural order by his own will or ingenuity – a very Athenian impulse – and loses everything he loves. The death of his son, Haimon, is the real tragic event of the play, not the death of Antigone. At best, there are two parallel, dissonant tragedies here, two characters who cannot change their minds, with Antigone the unwitting agent and Creon the dupe of the gods. So, it might even be time to feel sorry for the ageing Catholic congregations, who keep reaching for their PR companies and failing to understand. 'When the "Oh My God – mass grave in the West of Ireland" broke in an English-owned newspaper (*The Mail*) it surprised the hell out of everybody, not least the sister of the Bons Secours,' says Terry Prone of the Communications Clinic, who goes on to say that most of the nuns she represents are in their 80s now.

The Adoption Rights Alliance believes the state has a strategy of 'deny till they die': stalling until most birth mothers are dead. But though the children have gone away, there is a chance they will return. In *The Examiner* Conall O'Fatharta keeps breaking a story about Bessborough, another Mother and Baby home, also in Cork. A 2012 Health Service Report is concerned that 'death records may have been falsified so children could be brokered in clandestine adoption arrangements at home and abroad'. O'Fatharta says that according to figures given to the Public Health Inspector, 102 babies died there in 1942, a death rate of 82 per cent. There are, however, only 76 deaths on the order's own death register, and this pattern is repeated in the surrounding years. Where are the missing children? They may be alive, in America, old. If the problem in Bessboro and perhaps in Tuam was one, not of murder, neglect, or the discarded dead, but one of baby trafficking, few people in Ireland would be surprised. One day we will all wake up and be shocked by it, but not yet. Meanwhile, the Sisters of the Sacred Hearts of Jesus and Mary may, in the interests of respectability, decline to open their archives, except on their own terms.

In July, the Adoption Information and Tracing Bill was discussed in Cabinet. It will give as many as 50,000 adoptees the right to their birth certificate, if they promise not to contact their mothers, first. 'What we want,' says Susan Lohan of the Adoption Rights Alliance, is 'our file and nothing but the file'.

In August, shortly before the reburial of Thomas Kent, Dr Buckley, the Bishop of Cork and Ross, called for the exhumation of little Nellie Organ from the graveyard of Sunday's Well in Cork. Nellie was a wonderfully pretty little girl who suffered a long illness, and a terrible death – probably from tuberculosis – in the infirmary of the orphanage there. She died in 1908, at the age of 4. She was the darling of the nuns, and of all who came in contact with her. She received the host on her last day, and Irish schoolchildren were often told she died of happiness. Her story inspired Pope Pius X to lower the age of communion for children, from 12 to 7. The Bishop calls her the unofficial saint of the city. She was buried in St Joseph's Cemetery but was exhumed and reburied within the convent grounds 'at the nuns' request' Dr Buckley said. At the time of the exhumation, a year after Nellie's death, her remains were found to be intact. Nellie Organ is currently buried in the locked nun's plot at Sunday's Well, her grave is made distinctive, among the low plain crosses, by a large statue of the Infant of Prague. The Sunday's Well complex is now derelict. It is currently the property of Ulster Bank and of the accountancy firm KPMG.

THE HOTEL

By that time she had flown from Dublin to New York, then over to Milan for a disastrous day followed by a long trot down to Gate 74 where nothing was happening, there were no passengers, just a single, slightly accusatory air hostess who said the flight had been cancelled since yesterday: she would have to route through – and here her mind blanked, the way you blank the name of a person at a party – although some part of her brain must have known, because she turned and walked back the way she had come, past the Segafredo franchise, the Swatch counter, past two Italian men shopping for sunglasses at a little spinning stand, down to the new gate, the number of which was circled on her boarding pass. And it must have been written somewhere, this new destination in Germany, or Switzerland, or Austria (the signs, when she landed, were all in German), she just forgot it, she must have forgotten it several times, she was too busy hating Italian airlines in her head, maybe all Italians, her mind kept snagging on that cancelled flight, those two handsome men turning to admire their own reflection in the other's dark glasses. When they landed on the other side she followed the other passengers up an escalator down a glass walled corridor over and back along an empty baffle. She showed her passport to a tired official sitting high in a cubicle who did not ask if she knew what country she was trying to get into, so late at night. There should be a sign, she thought. A few bags circled on the carousel, but she left them to it, and walked between bare steel tables, out through the sliding doors into this new place.

The last few passengers walked around her towards the big revolving doors: men, going home to warm beds while she stood looking at a hotel voucher and a boarding pass for a flight that would leave in four hours' time. Or in five hours. Sometimes her smartphone took a little while to catch up with the time zone, but she was pretty sure the flight would leave in five hours, minus one hour's check in time. Boarding 05.55 from Gate 19. She should be back here, in the airport, in four hours exactly.

When she looked up from her calculations, the exit door had stopped revolving. The lights were switched off, you could not see the edges of the huge hall, and there was no one to ask which way to go. No cleaners, no security, no passengers pulling luggage or pushing trolleys in hijabs or shorts or travelling shawls. No announcements were being made. The airport was closed. Even the voice of the revolving door was silent, the one that warned you in alternating – in revolving – languages not to push the door. She checked each sign in turn until she came to the one she was looking for: a stick figure lying in a narrow bed, with 'Hotel' written underneath, then repeated in another language, which must have been French, 'Hôtel'.

'OK OK OK,' she said under her breath as she pulled her faithful trolley bag past a row of deserted car rental stands. 'OK OK OK' as she walked along a dotted line of stilled travelators wondering which direction they moved, when they went. Far ahead, a churning signalled one of them obstinately rolling past its bedtime. As she got closer she could see the stainless-steel walkway moving, and the black rubber handrail moving, but they seemed to be sliding in different directions and her foot was almost on the thing before she realised it was coming against her. She jinked to the side and made her way upstream towards another sign, pointing left, and another corridor, with a curved roof, like the fuselage of a plane, and this one was so long you could not see the end of of it. There were travelators on both sides now, and all of them were dead. She could hear the rasp of her coat sleeve against her coat and the regular clicking of her faithful roller between floor tiles: *ka thock ka thock ka thick*. There were no more signs.

Far away a travelator lurched into action and she startled, so the click of her roller wheels rent out of synch. It was like a keychange: *ka thick, ka thick, ka thick* against the distant low hum of the machine. The darkness of the corridor yielded two men, jolting a little as they were conveyed along like toy men – or toy soldiers – indeed, because they wore peaked caps and one of them had a large gun which he held across his front with both hands. The men stepped off the walkway and walked to the next, which came to life, even as the one behind them slowed. Perhaps she could do the same. She could fire one of these things up, sail past the soldiers as they sailed along the other side. But there was a gun. And she was not sure the machine would start for her. The policemen proceeded from one to the next. Their hats were white, and they had light green shirts under dark green flak jackets. When they got on to the walkway beside her she stopped on the motionless floor and waited for them to pass. The men turned slightly as they were conveyed beyond her.

'Hotel?' she said.

One of them laughed a little, the one with the gun. The other indicated over his shoulder, in the direction they had come.

'Ein bisschen weiter. You must go a little further.'

'Thank you,' she said, thinking, the accent was so soft, she must be somewhere south, she might have landed in Switzerland.

At the end of the corridor there was a set of glass doors, and beyond these the night air, bold orange street lamps, lighting starkly shadowed bushes, a deserted blue road and, on the other side of it, a big, beautiful hotel – she could imagine it: the feel of carpet under her roller wheels, dark wood, huge flowers scenting the air, a receptionist to say there will be a shuttle to departures from 5 am. A shower. A bed.

Or not a hotel. The building was a warehouse, or a kind of hanger. That was also possible. She closed her eyes for a moment, then opened them again, *Ka thick ka thick ka thick,* putting one foot in front of the other on the heavy-seeming floor. The doors were in front of her now. They would open when she was very near. She would pass through them into the night air and, across the road, a smiling woman behind a counter, a keycard to press against a numbered door, a little light that clicked green.

Or no hotel. Outside, across the road, was just another queue she had to join, a straggling line of people with their bags and some of them were sitting down, this time on the concrete of the street, where weeds grew out of the cracks, and men in green uniforms walked two by two, tapping the stock of their guns as if to reassure their HK 416Cs. As if to tell their HK 416Cs to wait, wait, that they were still here. And this line of people is wearing too many clothes, they have overcoats and cheap parkas, cardigans on top of cardigans, they have bits of cloth dangling off them, scarves and shawls, and one of them is wearing a blanket, which is not clean.

Outside the door there is no hotel, no numbered door that opens on a bed where she can sit and then lie back prising one shoe off with the toe of the other foot, so that one shoe and then the other shoe drops to the floor. No pillow she can roll her face on to, and then roll back, afraid she might fall asleep right there, afraid she might even drool. No. There is just this line of people who need a shower, and there is no shower, you can see it in their faces, there is no hope of water, let alone soap, let alone the cubicle she has been craving so hard, the beige stone walls and a granular, slip free floor, a flat shower rose big as the bottom of a bucket, the soap that smells of bergamot, orange blossom, green tea. There is just rubbing your face so the dirt comes off in needle thin rolls of black dust mixed with old sweat, and the smell is the settled smell when you have been through dirty and out the other side – a week after, a month after – when you are no longer rank, just stale. Because the line has been there for a long time, waiting to get into the shelter of the building that is across the road, a square block, that does not look like a shelter, apart from the fact of a roof. And inside this building with its high small windows, there is of course, another line, and more smiling soldiers, who are sometimes a little disgusted by the smell, and sometimes a little pissed off, sometimes bored, patting their gunstocks impatiently because you are anxious and slow. Because you need to go to the toilet, and that means leaving the line, which is such a hassle, and sometimes when you come back to the line there is actual human shit on you somewhere, on your shoe or the hem of your coat, because there is no money, there is no necessity, in the circumstances, to clean the toilet floor.

Beyond the automatic door there is no smiling receptionist in a quietly cut suit of hotel blue, to say that yes her flight is on schedule, the shuttle will be there at five, plenty of time; because the airport – whatever town they are in – is really quite small. And oh, breakfast does not start till six, so there will be croissants in the lobby. There will be no croissants, she knows that now. Outside the door, there is no vending machine for the people in the line, to spiral out a Twix or a bottle of water, and where is your passport? It does not matter. Where is your boarding card? Oh dear that does not apply, that boarding card, what a shame, it is not fit for purpose anymore. And the babies are crying, now, so never mind the croissants, she just needs to get through this line, all these people layered up in their cheap clothes, who are so shuffling, and slow, and she unzips her trolley for her travelling shawl because it is cold. And instead of a receptionist there is a man with a gun who is so bored, he is out of his mind with boredom. He adjusts his crotch to the left, hoists his belt, he has to shake out the hand that is clutching the stock of his gun, and he checks out the tits of the women in line, he is just checking tits all night, because he is so bored he just wants to fuck somebody now. He pushes a girl, when he is moving her along. Just a small shove, and it is important not to catch this man's eye, it is really important to keep looking at the floor. So never mind the cotton sheets, she just wants the soft gaze of her own man, the soft gaze of her son. She just wants to kiss her mother, because she is afraid her mother is in the line somewhere up ahead, in the sleeping block, perhaps, that is beyond this block, sitting on a bunk bed, or in the endless line that stretches out along the chain link fence, a line that lasts for weeks and months and years. And her mother is very patient but she is also old.

She is so close to the doors, she is afraid she will bang into the glass. She is afraid they will not open, and she is afraid of what is on the other side. The hotel was just a joke and she is lost. Because she does not know the name of the country she is in, and she no longer believes in home.

MAEVE BRENNAN:
GOING MAD IN NEW YORK

'TO BE AROUND HER ... WAS TO SEE STYLE BEING REINVENTED.'

Maeve Brennan's didn't have to be a woman for her work to be forgotten, though it surely helped. She did not have to become a bag lady for her work to be revived, though that possibly helped too. The story of her mental decline is terrifying for anyone who works with words, who searches her clean, sour sentences for some hint or indication of future madness, and then turns to check their own.

Brennan is, for a new generation of Irish women writers, a casualty of old wars not yet won. The prose holds her revived reputation very well, especially the Irish stories. These feel transparently modern, the way that Dubliners by Joyce feels modern. It is partly a question of restraint. Benedict Kiely, Walter Macken, perhaps even Mary Lavin, ran the risk of being 'Irish' on the pages of the New Yorker, which is to say lyrical, or endearing. Frank O'Connor was the cutest of the lot, perhaps, as well as the most successful. Brennan remains precise, unyielding: something lovely and unbearable is happening on the page.

Despite the lack of surface charm, Brennan was very Irish indeed. Her mother, Una, took part in the fighting at Easter 1916 alongside her father, Bob, who was arrested and sent to prison for it. Maeve was born 37 weeks later: conceived along with the Irish State you might say, she was a true daughter of The Rising. A few years later Bob Brennan left his young family to take part in the War of Independence and in the Irish Civil War. He spent months in hiding and on the run, and Maeve's childhood home was raided several times by men carrying guns. After the State was founded, he set up the Irish Press for Éamon de Valera, and in 1933, when Maeve was 17 her father was appointed to Washington as Ireland's first minister to America. The Brennan's could not have seen this remarkable future when they fell in love in the Gaelic League in Wexford, but they both saw some great ideal. Their three girls were named after ancient Irish Queens: Emer, Deirdre and Maeve.

She was a 'Gaelic Princess'. Her hair was chestnut, her eyes were green. A 'pixie', a 'changeling', she was admired for the sharpness of her wit. It is hard to find a description of Brennan that is not code for her ethnicity. In 1941 she moved to New York and found a job at *Harpers' Bazaar* and when her family returned to Ireland, she stayed behind; a 'traveller in residence'. Already reclusive, she moved from one rented room to another, and rarely had a kitchen to call her own. Still, she seemed to miss some idea of Ireland, or of domesticity. Her biographer Angela Bourke writes that: 'Throughout her adult life, to the point of eccentricity, Maeve drank tea and sought out open fires.'

In 1949, at the age of 32, she secured a staff job at the *New Yorker* where she had the great good fortune to be edited by William Maxwell, who became a loyal friend. 'To be around her,' he wrote, 'was to see style being reinvented.' Brennan was a beautiful, unmarried woman in a dingy office full of men. She wore a fresh flower in her lapel and smelt of Cuir de Russie, a perfume designed by Chanel for women who dared to smoke in public. She worked all the time, produced very little, and ate boiled eggs, to keep her figure neat.

By the early 1950s the descriptions of her Irishness had tipped from fey to fierce. Her tongue 'could clip a hedge', she had, 'a longshoreman's mouth', she said 'fuck' in company and drank in Costellos on 3rd Avenue. Once, when nobody came to take her order as she sat in a booth there, she lifted a heavy, full sugar bowl and dropped it on the floor. There was no sense, when she married her *New Yorker* colleague, St Clair Kelway, fellow drinker – fellow madman, indeed – that he was taking a virgin Irish bride. Brennan was 36. 'They were,' a friend said, 'like two children out on a dangerous walk: both so dangerous and charming.'

It is worth saying that no middle-class Irish woman at the time would set foot in a Dublin pub. Irish drinking culture, for all its famous good fun, was deeply shame-bound. Maeve's thirst had its origins in a terrific social uncertainty but also in a great want. As her posthumous editor Christopher Carduff said, her worked showed 'a ravenous grudge, a ravenous nostalgia and a ravenous need for love'.

Brennan's progress as a fiction writer was far from steady. She wrote a column of city observations as 'The Long-Winded Lady', and short pieces of memoir, in the sad, bright tone the *New Yorker* did so well. Her first published stories were lightly satirical and set in America. These were published between 1952 and 1956, after which came silence. The Irish stories, on which her reputation was revived, did not start to appear until 1959, a year after her mother's death, when her marriage had fallen apart. There was a second rush, of more hopeful fictions, after the death of her father in 1964.

The stories involve two couples the Bagots and the Derdons, who live in Ranelagh, where Brennan grew up. The Bagots are happier than the Derdons, but it can be hard to distinguish the memoir pieces from the fiction and one couple from another – they are all so lonely and their compass so small. They live, interchangeably, in Brennan's childhood home at 48 Cherryfield Avenue, they climb the same little stairs and look out on the same laburnum tree. The stories are painful acts of reclamation. Brennan circles around the few events of these people's lives. A new sofa arrives at the house, to great excitement. A man selling apples knocks at the door. People get married, they walk in the park, go to work and die. There are visits, disappointments and interminable, small cruelties – especially between the Derdons, whose only son John becomes a priest, leaving his mother bereft. Some of the most affecting stories are almost entirely without incident. A man goes into his dead wife's bedroom and finds nothing there. A woman sees her own shadow on the wall of her children's room and is comforted by it.

In the 1950s, there was nothing to indicate, as you read a *New Yorker* piece, whether it was true or made up, and the writers name, if it was given, came at the end. This put a wonderful pressure on the sentences, and the order in which they happened. A high value was placed on precision and physical detail; revelation came slow and in a low key. The culture of the pages may add to the feeling that Brennan is always starting out, somehow. Some of the pieces, as Maxwell observes, stay slight. They are, however, 'definitely stories, written with great care and radiant with the safety and comfort of home.' (This was a nice thing to say, but there is little comfort in the story of the Derdons, who annoy each other to death, almost, never mind the nice warm fires and the many cups of tea.)

A collection of The Long-Winded Lady's columns was published in 1969 and reviewed in *The Atlantic* by John Updike. At 52, Brennan was neither the impeccable style queen of her youth, nor the mad woman of her old age. She was 'a woman of legendary but fading Irish beauty, spectacular red hair and marvelously eccentric intelligence' or so said the writer William MacPherson, who was, at a guess, also drinking at that lunch. A collection of stories was also published that year under the slightly whimsical title, 'In and Out of Never Never Land'. This was well received but did not make it across the Atlantic, or into paperback. It was a promising start, in publishing terms, for a career that was already over.

In her *New York Times* review of this collection Anne O'Neill Barna wrote about how hard it could be to tell Irish writers apart: 'The intoxicating mention of Dublin street names ... or of country counties and towns, with their surges of inhibition and passion ... could have been the possession of any of the *New Yorker* Irish Writers.' It must have been suffocating to be so mixed up like that, especially for Brennan, who was obsessed with the particularity of things.

She was a Dublin writer, there are no rural cadences rolling through her prose. She was, besides, impatient of 'the bog and thunder variety of stuff that has been foisted abroad in the name of Ireland.' The Irish oral tradition has a performative aspect that can tip a writer's persona into 'personality', but Brennan's characters had very little 'character' to speak of. Even the word 'voice' caused her anxiety.

Brennan is described by those who knew her as stylish or Irish and they seem to know what these terms mean, but she is also described as either silent or voluble, and it is hard to reconcile the two. Perhaps she was like her mother. When Maeve brought her husband home in 1957 Una, who had long suffered bad health, was changed: 'instead of the pale, patient and suffering cipher that used to confront people, McKelway has seen only a bad little woman who hisses like a cat, laughs like a fiend, and chatters from morning to night telling interminable stories ... none (of them) containing, as McKelway said, a good word about <u>anyone</u>.'

In 'The Clever One', a piece about her own childhood, her sister Derry was 'always with me and always silent, while I talked endlessly.' Silent but ruthless – the young Maeve announces that she wants to become an actress, and Derry says, 'Don't go getting any notions into your head.' These memoir pieces circle around ancient difficulties and refuse to move on. Maeve is wrongly accused of mouthing the words at choir practise, and is obliged to sing in front of the whole school as punishment, but when she opens her mouth, only a dreadful cawing comes out – proof, if it were needed, of the Devil at work in her.

'Why couldn't you have kept your mouth shut,' her mother says in 'The Lie', a strange non-story that works like a negation of Frank O'Connor's classic 'First Confession'. Maeve breaks her sister's sewing machine in a fit of envy, and confesses the sin, along with the fact that she lied to her mother about it. But there is no absolution, no victory over the maddening sister. Speech itself is the mistake.

Long after Una died, Brennan told Maxwell how she longed to find her mother's voice again. It was: 'the voice you can say anything in… infinite, always changing, endlessly responsive, and capable of containing anything, and everything.' She also said it was the voice she heard in a Mozart symphony, which is a big description for a small woman, even if she was her mother.

Maeve's letters, that end anguished and delusional, start witty and sad. In 1959 a reader wrote to the magazine asking if any more of her stories were on their way and Brennan wrote a fake reply, 'I am terribly sorry to have to be the first to tell you that our poor Miss Brennan died. She shot herself in the back with the aid of a small handmirror at the foot of the main altar in St Patrick's Cathedral one Shrove Tuesday. Frank O'Connor was where he usually is in the afternoons, sitting in a confession box pretending to be a priest.'

O'Connor was by this time, a mainstay of the magazine. He often wrote about priests; he felt the loneliness of their vocation echoed that of the writer. Brennan was not so enthusiastic. When Father John Derdon comes back to his family home, 'the black cloth gave him a bad air', and his priesthood (whatever that is) is not entirely believed. 'There was something thin and jaunty about him, in the tilt of his head, or in one of the conscious, unnecessary gestures he was always making, that belonged more to an actor than to a priest.'

The later stories are occupied by the idea of 'notions', with the sense that people are not made foolish by their desires so much as fraudulent. In her long story, 'The Springs of Affection', Min cannot believe her twin brother wants to leave to get married. 'It was as though a bad trick had been played on them all.' Even Martin seems to sense it: he stops outside the church to say, 'I feel like a great stranger all of a sudden.' The whole family is devalued, when he goes. 'Instead of being reflections of Martin they became copies of one another or three not very fortunate copies of a face that was gone.' The love he has for Delia, his new bride, is of no consequence. Because Min cannot tell herself apart from her brother, his marriage brings sex, or the idea of sex, into the family, where it does not belong. Delia Kelly, with her 'queer, cloud green eyes' is 'making free with a part of Min Bagot'. No wonder the wedding feels 'unnatural'. It puts Min in an agony of self consciousness and she is subject to new confusions. Delia's family 'didn't talk, as (she) understood talk ... The dead were mentioned with the same voice as the living.'

Anxiety about madness runs through 'The Springs of Affection'. Delia may have 'queer' eyes, but her aunt Mag, being too fond of a tree, is fully 'queer'. Min's own father, whom she holds in contempt, is also described as queer, and her sister Clare takes after him – 30 years after the wedding, Min feels 'obliged' to have her 'locked up in the Enniscorthy lunatic asylum'. Perhaps it is the effort to stay sane that makes Min vicious. There is no tenderness in her, even as a girl. 'Min despised her father,' Brennan writes, 'but she hoped her mother wouldn't hit him.' It is hard to think of another Irish writer who would put such a flat and finished thought into the mind of a child.

The appalling thing, or the strange thing, is the way her brother agrees with Min in the end. Decades later, after she is dead, Min says, 'There was nothing to Delia,' and Martin says, 'Nothing to Delia. That's true.' Later adding, 'That's a weight off my mind.' The two are happy in their childhood state the way Min, after Martin's death, is happy to possess all his things.

Looked at one way, Min's circling envy, her paranoia and incestuous fury is close to madness. Viewed through another lens, it is just the Irish family – or any family – doing its thing. The story exists on the edge of psychosis. Both sex and death undo Min's sense of personal circumference: Martin is the same as Min, the dead are the same as the living. The only sign that the writer might be inside the problem rather than outside it, is the mad way that Martin agrees with Min's madness. Even so, the story manages not to swallow itself, somehow. Min is surrounded, in her little flat, by her possessions and her siblings' possessions. Things provide a kind of sanity, for being external and real. Brennan's work anchors itself time and again in the objects of her childhood: a certain carpet, her mother's potted ferns, a sofa, bits and pieces of china.

It is hard, however, to tell people apart. In one of her saddest columns The Long-Winded Lady observes a drunk woman, respectably dressed, trying to cross the road on Broadway. There is something over-lit about the scene, 'the deep-dyed neon rays of red and green and blue and white gave each face in the crowd a family likeness, so we all seemed to be related – dubious, discoloured copies of one another.' Una and her three daughters were 'the four faces of a personality'. To leave your family was to be diminished, sundered. How can you separate from something that is also yourself?

Mrs Derdon's anguish at the loss of her son John may mirror Una's grief at the loss of her daughter to America. If so, it was a terrible thing. 'There was no one for her to look at, except Hubert, and Hubert could turn into a raving lunatic, frothing and cursing, and there would be no one to see him except herself.' By his own account Bob Brennan suffered a breakdown in 1921 and again in 1922, under the pressure of the fight for Independence, and it is possible that Una had her problems too. Maeve expressed huge guilt about leaving her family, but it does not seem to inhere in the usual things – sex, religion or lifestyle. Her biggest sin is writing itself.

In 1963 she writes from Dublin: 'The pain radiated by the Envious One is terrible to endure. The pain that envious people feel, it is frightful, it must be. And this shame I feel all my life – I was as ashamed of having a little talent as another would be of being born without a nose.'

The 'Envious One' is her father, Bob Brennan, who is, like his daughter, a writer. Over the years, has sent her his unpublished stories as well as published books and Maeve is
convinced he is jealous of her success. This may be true – Bob might be a bit mad – or it might be a mad thing to say. Already, in this letter, she cannot distinguish between his pain and her own.

If you look at the Irish women who made it into the lists after Brennan, many of them were some man's daughter. Jennifer Johnston's father was the playwright Denis Johnston. Julia Ó'Faoláin is the daughter of Sean Ó'Faoláin. Eavan Boland is the daughter of another Irish ambassador – this time to the UK – and all of these women wrote at a time when few women made it on to the published page. Many of them were, like Mary Lavin, born and educated abroad. The sons of writers did not survive their Oedipal impossibilties to imitate this trend.

If Bob Brennan was jealous of his daughter, he must have been keenly aware of Frank O'Connor who, like him, had been involved in the fight for Independence – they worked together on *The Cork Examiner* in 1922. O'Connor grew famous in Ireland, a country where Maeve remained completely unknown. He was, for a while, manager of the Abbey Theatre and some of his work was banned by the Irish Censorship Board. By the time he was invited to lecture at Harvard in 1952 his reputation was secure both at home and abroad.

Publishing in the *New Yorker* might enhance a reputation at home, but it could not make one. The country, still deeply impoverished post-war, remained wary of foreign influence and jealous of foreign success. Maeve Brennan may also have managed that female trick of being both well regarded and completely unimportant, one that played out in America often enough - though, the deafness to the female voice in Ireland made these issues of reputation moot in her native land. No one here seemed to notice her enough to judge her worth one way or the other.

On the same day they reviewed her short stories in 1969, the *New York Times* led with a long piece about Philips Roth's 'Portnoys Complaint'. They also reviewed Simone de Beauvoir, as well as diaries and recollections by Ann Bridge, Lesley Blanch and Cynthia Asquith. In the main pages there were more books by women than men reviewed, and some of those names endured. In the corresponding Saturday edition of the *Irish Times* the books reviewed were all by men. None of them are now well known (E. V. Cunningham, anyone?). It is as though an aversion to the female voice bent the critics towards forgettability. Ireland was deaf to more than women, clearly; but it was also deaf to women, and it is inconceivable that Brennan could have been reviewed here in 1969. It is a miracle she made it in 1998; the paper was still blithely publishing male only book pages in 2013. The silence of the more Catholic newspapers, including the *Irish Press*, is a sadder tale.

No Irish paper published an obituary when she died in 1993, in a nursing home where no one knew her history, not even Brennan herself. 'I write every day in the *Irish Press* and get paid', she wrote in one of her last letters. A perfect life, clearly. The *New Yorker* never happened. She was back on the pages her father had made.

In 1997, Christopher Carduff published *The Springs of Affection* – this volume of her Dublin stories – in America, and they were warmly endorsed by Alice Munro and Edna O'Brien. She was introduced to the Irish public by Fintan O'Toole, then an arts columnist for the *Irish Times*, in January 1998. Brennan was 'one of the children of the revolution' he said, who, by the end, 'more or less lived in the women's toilets in the *New Yorker* building.' He found in her work, 'a vague but powerful anxiety about how women's lives could get lost.'

Angela Bourke's landmark biography came out in 2004. It was a great work of literary reclamation, and Brennan's reputation as an Irish writer was set. The image of Brennan as lost or discarded, destitute and psychotic, was offset by iconic photographs taken by Karl Bissinger, of a beautiful, distant woman. Feminist editor, Sinéad Gleeson laments the current interest in Brennan's: 'vintage wardrobe and fabulous up-dos, as opposed to the world she created on the page.'

Roddy Doyle's mother, Ita, is Brennan's cousin and he remembers a long visit she made to the family in Kilbarrack, when she was sober, hard-working, completely normal. Some of Brennan's surviving relatives wrote to complain to the *Irish Times* when she was depicted on the Project stage as 'foul-mouthed'. They never heard her swear, they said. 'She may have picked up some vulgar language at the *New Yorker*, but it would not have been part of her Irish heritage.'

The house at 48 Cherryfield Avenue was part of a new suburb when Una and Bob moved there in 1921. This was a time when a certain kind of Irish life became set in bricks and mortar, and the house still exists just as described. There is a small, provisional looking shop on the corner, a commercial garage abutting the back wall, and a sports' ground beyond. It is possible the laburnum tree still blooms in the garden. My mother's family lived in a mirroring terrace on the Northside of the city, a slightly bigger house in the less affluent suburb of Phibsboro. The walnut furniture described in the title story of '*The Springs of Affection*' matches the furniture my grandmother bought at around the same time the Brennans set up home. I spent 40 years looking at the veneer, and not looking at the bed where my mother's siblings were conceived and, many decades later, laid out. When Brennan's work was republished in the 1990s, I did not think of her as beautiful or lost. I thought of her as being from these new suburbs: the world on the page as familiar and horrible as your own foot. As with Dubliners, the language moves through the stasis of her characters' lives with a beautiful and painful precision. Each one of Brennan's stories is a victory over sameness and the loss of meaning. She makes a bid for her sanity, one sentence at a time.

SOLSTICE

It was the year's turning. These few hours like the blink of a great eye – just enough light to check the world is still there, before shutting back down.

Some time in the mid-afternoon, he had an impulse to go home, or go somewhere, and when he lifted his head, of course it was dark outside. It just felt wrong. Two hours later, he was in the multi-story looking for his car, and he couldn't find the thing. It was like a lost dog. He clicked the key fob over and over, but there were no answering lights flashing orange on Level 2, where he usually parked, or on Level 3. He went up the little stairs to Level 4, then along the tiny path on the side of the ramp to 4A, brushing against the live cars, that were stuck on the slope, nose to tail. He glanced into the windows as he went past and there was a gone look to the drivers faces; they'd already left for home.

Out there, it was Christmas, but he did not think it was Christmas inside the multi-story, the only place in Dublin that had no fairy lights. He walked the last ramp to Level 5. Above him, the black concrete angles of the car park roof gave way to the night sky, and the car was right there, out in the weather. He took a moment to glance up and around him at the longest night of the year.

It felt like the end of things. Made you want your religion back. He looked out over the landscape of west Dublin, the square industrial units set among dark young trees, and he entertained the possibility that it would not work this time. This time, the world would spin deeper into shadow. And because the exit ramps were still jammed, he stayed a minute to check the solstice on his phone. For some reason it didn't always happen on the same day, but in 2016 it came just when you thought it should, on the 21st of December. Not at midnight though – 'the event', as the website called it, would happen at 10.44 am Irish time. Somewhere in that moment, whether he believed it or not, the sun would pause in the sky above him, or seem to pause. It would stop in its descent and start its slow journey back to summer and the middle of the sky.

Or this year, he thought, it might not bother.

The M50 was at a crawl, and there was the usual nightmare getting off at the Tallaght exit. He could see the red taillights running in a sequence towards him until he pushed his own brake pedal down. It would be stop-start all the way to Manor Kilbride.

A full 40 minutes later, the dual carriageway turned into the old Blessington Road and oncoming traffic shot by so close he flinched in the glare of the lights. This was the part of the journey that he loved best: the streetlamps gave way to the idea of countryside, and there was a song on the radio as the road opened up ahead. The music made him feel like he could keep driving forever. It was a love song, or a sad song. It reminded him of a time in his life, some town he was in, he could not say where. The loss of that place made him unsure of this one. Or indifferent – as though he could clip an oncoming car and it wouldn't matter. And he didn't know what he was thinking, until a truck bellied past, sucking the air from the side of the car.

It gave him a fright. He checked all the mirrors and shifted in his seat, set his hands more deliberately on the steering wheel. After the turnoff, he followed his own headlights down a country lane, and when he got to the house he sat in the parked car for quite a while.

The night was very big, out here.

There were three texts on his phone; ten, fifteen minutes apart.

When home?

Will I put yr name in the pot?
Food anyway, half seven.

When he comes in the door, there is the smell of cooking, the sound of pans and of water pouring into the sink. His daughter is failing to set the table and complaining about the Dakota Access pipeline. 'It's, like, so unfair,' she says, and her family neither agrees or disagrees, because that's just asking for it. Ruth is 15. She is arguing with her own shadow, her mother, her teachers, none of whom care about the Dakota Access pipeline, or not enough for her. 'We live in County Wicklow,' as her mother sometimes likes to remind her. But Ruth does not see what *location* has to do with anything, and he would admire this more, he might even take up the discussion, but she is back on her phone.

He glances over her shoulder and, for once, she lets him see.

'What's that?'

'Just,' she says. A person called chikkenpenis has sent a funny picture to do with Kanye's breakdown, a video clip that jerks and repeats, endlessly. It's hard to know what the joke is. And what kind of person spells 'penis' right and 'chicken' with two 'ks'?

'Is that someone you know?'

Ruth just rolls her eyes, types with two thumbs. Cracks up laughing, saying, 'Oh, my God. Oh, my God!'

He looks into the kitchen, where his wife is trying to serve up stir fry, out of a too-heavy pan. She is in her track pants. Upstairs all day, at a guess, translating some car manual for solid German euroes. Her hair is in a scrunchie, which does not suit her. He tries to remember the song he heard on the radio as he goes over to help, but 'Go, go. Out!' she says and it is gone.

Halfway through dinner he becomes aware that Ross, his son, is talking to him about something or someone called Stripey. His son says that Stripey knew about death because he always went to Tiger's grave. After a moment he realises Stripey is a cat and so is Tiger. The ones at the child-minder's, when he was little. Cats from many years ago.

'Animals believe in death,' his son says.

'You think?'

This is a big statement, for a ten-year-old.

'Maybe he was just waiting for the other cat to come back out of there. I mean, maybe he doesn't know what the ground is. Maybe he doesn't believe in the ground.'

The boy's face goes still, and he looks at his plate,

Ruth goes, 'Kcchchhhh', does a Carrie hand out of the grave. And there is an immediate fight. Shouting, pushing.

'Hey hey, that's enough,' he says.

When they are settled, his wife casts a baleful look at him, and he shoots one back, *What have I done now?*

'I think the the cat was sad,' she says to Ross. 'I think Stripey missed Tiger, don't you?'

She has put her hand on the loose fist his own hand makes beside his plate. This is one of the things they fight about. *Stop undermining your own son.* Which irritates the hell out of him. Because the boy has to learn how to roll with the punches. 'Could have been hungry,' he says. 'Yum yum. Dead cat.'

Ruth starts to laugh. And Ross obliges him with a crooked smile.

His wife pushes back from the table; starts collecting the plates, though they are only just finished.

'Sorry that was so,' she says. 'It was just a rustle up.'

'Lovely,' he says.

Oh great, he thinks. On the longest night, his wife with that look in her eye that says, *Christmas is coming, and it is all turning to shite.*

Correction. His wife with a look that says, *Christmas is coming, and it is all your fault.*

He pours a glass of wine and almost spills it on himself falling asleep on the sofa after the news. He was dreaming about weather or discussing the weather with his dreaming self: all autumn it had been so dry, high pressure, clear skies, the leaves drying to dust on the trees, falling like smoke, they'd hung on so long. It occurs to him that Tiger was Stripey's mother. The cat's mother, no less. He says as much to his wife, who is sitting across the room. She looks at him.

'Yes,' she says. And he suddenly remembers that his own mother is dead – a fact he manages to forget for days at a time.

'You think they'd make a better go of the names,' he says.

Later, he mutes the TV to check on a noise, and hears his daughter singing upstairs. She has her headphones on, her voice half in her head, half in the room.

'Goddamn truck,' he says, 'Nearly had the wing mirror. You know the bend.'

'Be careful,' his wife says. 'This time of year, they're all drinking.'

'They're all wrecked,' he says, 'I was half asleep myself.' 'No, not asleep,' she looks a bit shocked. 'Just a bit.'

Unmoored. That is the word he is looking for. Recently he feels – he has felt – unmoored.   He used to have a place in his mind where he could go. Hard to say where it was, but his mother has been dead since April, so maybe this was the place she used to occupy. Because he can't go there anymore. It was the song that reminded him.

'I was listening to the radio,' he says.

'The radio?'

It wasn't like an inner monologue or anything, he did not sit around talking to his mother all day. It was more like a silence. He had lost a great and wonderful silence. The traffic came against him and he felt unprotected, bullied by the lights. Because he had no one on his side, anymore. Not even his wife.

'Yes, the radio. In the car. You know I wish, for once, you'd let me say something without repeating it back at me, like some kind of gom.'

She lets this sink in for a moment and then gets up out of the big armchair and leaves the room. He can hear the sound of her starting to unload the dishwasher.

And *Mutual*, he wants to shout after her, *Fucking Mutual*. He wants to tell her how he sat in the car, outside his own house, thinking: whatever happens when I walk in the door; that's the thing. When I walk in the door, I will find it. The answer or the question, one or the other. It will be there.

And what did he find?

These people.

This.

Even in her sleep she is affronted, her body straight in the bed beside him, her head twisted to face the wall. The earth spins them towards morning, and he cannot close his eyes for the vertigo; he has to urge it on. He wakes without knowing he has slept, and the house is busy around him – the sound of the front door, finally, and silence. It is after nine o'clock, but when he comes into the kitchen Ross is still at the table, stuck on his phone.

'It's the Christmas concert,' his son says, as if that explains something.

The office is closed but he still has a mad number of payments to process before the end of the year, so he takes a coffee back to bed and opens his laptop there. He clicks on a spreadsheet, then he starts reading the news instead and wandering about online.

Ross comes in to show him something. He climbs across the duvet, bringing the phone screen so close, his father has to push the thing a distance away. It is a photograph of two tigers, play-fighting in the Siberian snow.

They are pretty impressive, the tigers.

'Fantastic,' he says.

And Ross is so pleased, his cheeks glow with it.

It is 10.38 and outside, the sun has not cleared the top of the winter trees.

'Look up "solstice",' his father says, spelling it out for him and then typing it on his own keyboard because he is running out of time, now. He has six minutes to do this, to tell his child that the world will keep turning. No matter what happens, the sun will always rise in the morning, the planet's orbit will tilt them toward the light. He finds a video clip of a cartoon earth circling a harmless, small sun, but Ross already knows about the solstice, he says, they have covered it at school.

It is 10.42.

The boy is sitting cross-legged on the bed beside him. Ross shuts his eyes, and 'Sssh,' he says. 'Is it happening?'

'In a minute,'

'Is it now?'

The seconds pass. The boy squeezes his eyelids tighter.

'Now?'

'Yes.'

Ross keeps his eyes shut for another moment, then punches the air. He turns to his dad and they look at each other, full of mischief and amazement. Because it happened. Nothing happened, but they know it was there. The tiny stretch of daylight that will become summer.

His wife is home. She is standing in the doorway watching them. They look up and smile at her.

'What?' she says.

CALL YOURSELF GEORGE:
GENDER REPRESENTATION IN THE IRISH LITERARY LANDSCAPE

'THE CAT SAT ON THE MAT'

In 2015, the novelist Catherine Nichols sent the opening pages of the book she was working on to 50 literary agents. She got so little response she decided to shift gender and try as 'George' instead. The difference amazed her. 'Fully a third of the agents who saw his query wanted to see more, where my numbers never did shift from one in 25.' The words, as written by George, had an appeal that Catherine could only envy. She also, perhaps, felt a little robbed. 'He is eight and a half times better than me at writing the same book.'

This was hardly a scientific study, but it is tempting to join in her conclusion that men and women are read differently, even when they write the same thing. So, if a man writes 'The cat sat on the mat' we admire the economy of his prose; if a woman does so we find it banal. If a man writes 'The cat sat on the mat' we are taken by the simplicity of his sentence structure, its toughness and precision. We understand the necessary connection between cat and mat, sense the grace of the animal, admire the way percussive monosyllables sharpen the geometrics of the mat beneath. If the man is an Irish writer we ask, if the cat is, perhaps, Pangur Bán, the monk's cat from the 9th century poem of that name – the use of assonance surely point to the Gaelic tradition. In which case the mat is his monk's cell, a representation of life of the mind, its comforts and delineations. The cat, so female and probably white, is the secret sensuality of the ascetic life; not in the monastery garden, or out in the bog, but carefully and neatly sitting in its proper, bounded place. Or the mat is Ireland itself – if this is not too much of a reach – in the age of saints and scholars, that golden, undivided time before the Norman invasion, in which case, the cat could be anything at all. The cat is the playful cipher, sitting on a very inert, very territorial mat. No – scratch all that – this is just a very truthful, very real sentence (look at those nouns!). Containing both masculine mat and feminine cat, it somehow Says It All.

If, on the other hand, a woman writes 'The cat sat on the mat', her concerns are clearly domestic, and that is sort of limiting. Maybe it's time to go below the comments line and make jokes about pussy.

I am just kidding, of course. These are anxieties, projections, phantasmagoria – things to which women are particularly prone.

In the first week of 2013 I started to count, in an idling way, the number of books by women reviewed in the weekly arts pages of the *Irish Times* and found none. They were all by men. There was a short interview with a woman, Mary Costello, a writer whose sentences are notably clean and assured. Under her photograph a sub editor put the quote: 'I find the public side of being published very difficult.' A single subheading read, 'Shy and unassuming.'

A poem 'Women's Christmas' was also printed on one of the books pages. This was a translation of Seán Ó Ríordáin's 'Óiche Nollag na mBan' a feast day on the 6th January on which women traditionally gathered to socialise without men. 'There was a power in the storm that escaped last night, / last night on Women's Christmas / from the desolate madhouse behind the moon / and screamed through the sky at us, lunatic'

The following week I couldn't find, in four pages of book reviews, any discussion of a book by a woman. Perhaps I wasn't looking closely enough: a later search revealed that there were two single paragraphs in the paperback round-up. In the third week of January there was finally a substantial piece on a book not only by but also about a woman – Grace Coddington, who works in the fashion industry – as well as two paperback reviews. Work by or about women took up one half of four pages, or 12.5

per cent of the available space, that week, bringing the years total to less than 8 per cent.

Over the year, the figures for books written by women reviewed in the *Irish Times* rose to 29 per cent. Beside it on the news stand the *Irish Independent* had higher figures without much fuss, with a total of 37 per cent of books by women. In Sept 2013, the *Independent* even had an unheralded – possibly accidental – all-female review section.

The poem 'Women's Christmas', is actually about male anxiety, which made its publication to mark the day feel like a bit of a con. Once I noticed this sleight of hand it was hard to stop seeing it – the idea that women are somehow present when men write poems about them, or have them as characters in their books, or write about their role in Irish history. And this is so brilliantly hermetic, it made me wonder what disaster awaits, when you let women's actual voices in (screaming through the sky, lunatic).

In 2013, One City One Book, which promotes a single book throughout Dublin over the course of a month, announced for the eighth year in a row that its selection was by a man – although, of course this was not how it was phrased. If it had been so phrased, they might have noticed, because the next two choices were also books written by men, making for a ten year straight. Unlike a newspaper, this is a publicly funded programme. What were they thinking, the good people of the Dublin City Libraries and of the Unesco City of Literature? Hard to say.

A shift in the *Irish Times* was signalled in early 2015 by a series of articles in praise of Irish women writers, published online. A selection of these encomiums was published for Women's Day in March, and this was run on a double-page spread with a poster of female Irish Writers on the facing page: 'an antidote to the all-male Irish Writers poster of bars and student bedrooms.' This was an interesting hybrid, fed by the online discussions that have opened the critical conversation in recent years, but still asserted the old authoritarian style which liked to keep men and women separate.

In November 2015, the Abbey Theatre announced its schedule for the commemorative year of the 1916 Rising, which contained nine plays by men and one by a woman. Online criticism provoked an impulsive response from the then director of the theatre Fiach MacConghail ('Them's the breaks,' he tweeted, while running to catch a plane). This led to a gathering of hundreds of women in the theatre on 15th November to demand an explanation, which he bravely tried but failed to give. This movement, called Waking the Feminists, later compiled statistics on gender representation in Irish theatre, 2006–15, which found that the more funding it received the more male an institution became. The Abbey is the national theatre of Ireland and its programme was also skewed by the important, and clearly male, business of reflecting or defining the national consciousness; work started very deliberately by Yeats and Lady Gregory when they founded the theatre in 1904.

The argument about excellence – that women's work just isn't good enough – is incredibly hurtful, given that there is so much mediocre work by men around. Theatre is a high-stakes medium. Some of the Abbey plays I have seen over the years were wonderful, and some truly excruciating. I would fall out of the theatre afterwards thinking there was no point in being high-minded (though the Irish cultural discussion can be painfully high-minded), what we needed was more, or at least *some*, ghastly plays by women.

Perhaps the roasting of the theatre's director focused a few minds in the cultural community. Recently I went back to the newspapers to find the atmosphere had changed. The figures were up 10 per cent in the *Irish Times*, with a total of 39 per cent of books reviewed in 2016 written by women, and up 3 per cent at the *Irish Independent*, which despite some all-male weeks in October still came in ahead at 40 per cent.

This matches more or less what we know about the gender balance in published books. It is impossible to be definitive here. A study based on the online Hathi Trust Library shows that nearly 40 per cent of fiction is currently written by women. The percentage is lower in crime and higher in popular fiction. In nonfiction (of the kind that gets reviewed) women have a lower profile, but they do exist, probably around or under 20 per cent. The figure for all published books is often given at something over a third. When it comes to literary fiction, my sense of the market corresponds with what Ruth Franklin found in American publishing in 2010, when she pointed out that the gender ratios at 'the elite literary houses' were sharply different from those pitching to a broader audience, citing the gap between Random House US at 37 per cent and Knopf at 23 per cent.

Growing awareness and dissatisfaction with the situation have been fed by organisations like VIDA, an online resource for women in the literary arts, which started counting book reviews in 2010. This spring, to take one example, Vintage, which publishes paperbacks from eight imprints as part of Penguin Random House UK, had 38 per cent of books written by women on their contemporary list. Most Irish publishers have not, so far, engaged in the public discussion, but their current figures are far from terrible. New Island publishes fiction, non-fiction, poetry and crime. Their webpage lists 286 books, going back more than 20 years, and a pretty impressive 33.5 per cent of them are by individual women. This figure rises to 37 per cent of new releases. Lilliput Press, with smaller numbers, has increased publication of books by women from a, typically low 13 per cent in 2015 to 40 per cent this year. In 2016 Gallery Press had three titles by women out of a listed eight, a small sample (with the collected plays of Brian Friel counted as one), which nevertheless yields a ratio of 37.5 per cent. These numbers are far from parity, but they are certainly not excluding. Sampling of the figures, both in Ireland and internationally, makes anything over 40 per cent feel like a miracle and anything under 30 per cent a crime.

Everyone I spoke to in Irish publishing was alert to the issues, keen to catch a sense of change. There is a boom in small magazines: *Banshee*, with three women editors, is predominantly female. *Gorse* and *Winter Papers* come in around the half way mark. The *Stinging Fly*, founded in 1998 by Declan Meade and Aoife Kavanagh, moved quickly to parity and women writers were in a majority in 2016. The editor of the *Dublin Review*, Brendan Barrington, a constant advocate of 'that under-recognised creature, the Irish non-fiction writer' remains dissatisfied with the journal's gender balance, although it rose from 31 per cent in 2013 to 39 per cent last year.

The traditionally low numbers of women publishing in non-fiction begs many questions about the kinds of discourse we consider useful or true. We must be in possession of the facts. Without them we are dispossessed. In Ireland the question of ownership is not just about who owns the actionable present, however, but overwhelmingly about who owns the past, a place that remains unstable or unfinished, and one from which women tend to disappear.

Meanwhile, here in the present, it is hard to know how many women try to fix their voices in print. Most houses do not keep a gendered tally of submissions, but I could not draw the conclusion, from the tiny samples available in Ireland, that women were being turned away, en masse, from the door. Tramp Press, a highly successful feminist house, well known among aspiring writers for working their slush pile, reports 2,145 submissions since they were established in 2014 of which 818, or 'a disappointing 38 per cent', came from women.

Most books that make it into print don't come from the slush pile, they are commissioned or are submitted by agents who keep their processes confidential, and this is a significant gap in the numbers, in Ireland as elsewhere. Recently I walked into a shop in Dublin and counted the volumes in the Irish fiction section. Books by and about James Joyce took up 20 per cent of the shelf space and the weighty representation of Beckett, Wilde, Bram Stoker and Swift also skewed the figures towards a male past, but if you discount secondary or critical texts the numbers are surprisingly high: 290 books by women out of 671 fiction titles, that is, 43 per cent.

These numbers decline sharply when you move up the food chain. The main prize for the Irish Novel (now sponsored by The Bord Gáis Energy Awards) has been won ten times by men since 2003, and four times by women (28.5 per cent). Higher up again, the International Dublin Literary Award (formerly known as the Impac) is the richest on the literary landscape, with a purse of €100,000. This has been won by a man each year for the last 16 years.

The clumping of men at the top is such an international phenomenon, it is worth looking at how reviewing works in a country like Ireland, to see some of the dynamics at play – this apart from the complaints about condescension, small mindedness, envy and savagery that you hear everywhere, especially in places like Holland or New Zealand, that consider themselves in some way 'small'.

If you open out the figures for the *Irish Times* a more complex picture emerges. In 2013, 29 per cent of books reviewed were by women. This figure sank to 24 per cent of large, feature reviews (which also includes interviews) and rose to 32 per cent in regular reviews (800–150 words). It rose again, to 41 per cent in small reviews where books get less than 150 words apiece. So, although all of these books by women were worth noticing, they were not, in 2013, all worth noticing at length. More prominent coverage was afforded to male writers at a rate of three male writers to one female. This happened despite the fact that women wrote 41 per cent of the longer reviews.

Overall, there were many more women doing the reviewing than being reviewed. Women wrote nearly half the small pieces, and almost two thirds of the standard reviews. Editors sometimes say that it is hard to persuade women to write pieces, but this was clearly, in this category, not the case. The figures were not weighted by the fact that the paper's Literary Correspondent, Eileen Battersby, is a woman, as only around a quarter of the pieces she wrote that year were about female writers. Her Books of the Year page ran 18.5 per cent female, a low figure that can be partly explained by her focus on literature in translation, which, according to Rachel McNicholl of the Women in Translation movement, is 75 per cent male.

The most distinctive thing, to my mind, is the pattern of gender interactions. Of the regular and longer reviews, women reviewed 80 books by men, and men reviewed 28 books by women. This ratio of 2.7 to 1 is very much out of whack with the balance of reviewers, who were 53 per cent male. We can only guess at the reasons why men should not be asked to review books by women, or why they might decline.

The improvement in 2016, was not just in terms of numbers but also in terms of space allocated to books by women. The increase was not just seen in regular reviews which went up to 49 per cent female, it was also seen in larger, prestige pieces which ran two to one, male to female. Of reviewers, 49 per cent were male. The gender interactions, though more even, were still skewed. Men reviewed 48 books by women, while women reviewed 86 books by men: a ratio of 1.7 to 1. The story of women's role in the Rising was a dominant theme in the popular commemorations during the centenary year, and this new perspective owes much to the work of women historians, who are a minority in the field. Which makes you wonder why, on the Easter weekend, the then *Irish Times* literary editor, Fintan O'Toole, ran a full page about women of the Rising that was written by three men.

Ken Keating who compiled these figures on the *Irish Times* noted that the proportion of women reviewed dipped towards the end of the year. Perhaps this is a reflection of the work it takes to maintain gender balance – as many editors have claimed, both at home and abroad. The difficulty is often framed not as a problem 'for' women, but a problem 'about' women. Women are under confident, they don't step up, they lack self-belief. The female reviewers of the *Irish Times* clearly did step up, reviewing both men and other women, so just for two minutes, I would like to stop saying 'the problem with women is', and start looking in another direction.

Affinity is surely a joyful thing. I have often admired the ease with which men like books by other men, and envied, slightly, the way they sometimes got admired in their turn. This spiral of male affection twists up through our cultural life, lifting male confidence and reputation as it goes. Work by men is also read and discussed by female critics – only one side of the equation is weak, the lack of engagement with women's work by men.

There have been, in my lifetime, so many weird arguments about whether women were any good, as writers, whether they could ever be considered great, as writers, most of them started by snarling old men. Women found these arguments – so casually made – confusing, undermining, worth disproving. Vast amounts of work was undertaken, some by women in Irish universities. It always seemed to me a double burden, that women should suffer the discrimination and do all the work to fix it. (Besides, who are you trying to convince?)

In 1991 *The Field Day Anthology of Irish Literature* was published and, as everyone knows, they (mostly) forgot to put women in there. I was just starting out then as a writer and I would love to say that I was outraged, but I just felt contempt for the editors involved. I also felt a great sense of freedom. If you aren't going to be heard, then you can say what you like. This unmasking of false authority gave me a sense of childish delight. In the decade or so that followed I gleefully noted every time I was the only woman on the panel, every time I was interrupted on the panel, every time I was asked to go on a panel or read or speak 'because they had no women' because 'they needed a woman' because 'they forgot to get any women' or the more benign iterations of 'because they would love to hear a female voice'. I ran a private competition for 'worst introduction from an Irish male academic'; a close-run race, definitively won by a distinguished professor who was so drunk as to be incomprehensible, except for the phrase: 'we must forgive her for writing well'.

You never hear this guff from other writers, who are mostly interested in each other's sentences: the problem was always in the public realm, not on the shared privacy of the page. I was included in literary conversations in order to discuss women's exclusion from these conversations; and this did not happen outside Ireland, or at least not to me, but only at home.

I am happy to read both men and women, so I found it hard to explain an attitude I did not share. Nor did I know what these people wanted me to be. I realised that when they said 'woman' the word meant something to them that was hidden – from me certainly, but mostly from themselves. It was extremely tiresome. To be constantly reminded that you are female is to be pushed back into your body, over and over, when, as a writer, you do not function as a body, but as a voice.

I have met men, not just in Ireland, who are happy to say that they don't read women. They. Just. Can't.

There are so many problems 'with' women. They write about their feelings and not the facts (they take and do not give). They use qualifications, modifiers, metaphors. They go all fuzzy on you. It is not enough to connect – in fact connection is a fraught business – we must also establish distance, writing must clarify, not embroil. There is some anxiety in all this, not just about imagination, but about presence or disappearance, tangibility, possession.

There is also, and later, the problem that women were historically deemed weak, and weakness is something to be, on a personal level, expunged. The association of women with contamination is possibly more fundamental than the problem of feminisation; the fact that some men can't be caught reading a novel in case their friends call them a pussy. It also precedes male anxieties about female anatomy, which are often anxieties about their own anatomy, especially its penetrability. Perhaps this is why I am asked what it is 'like' to be a woman, as if the female condition were some kind of mystery beyond the power of men to understand.

There are many things to consider, before the question, in Ireland, becomes one about Catholic repression, or the drama of sexual attraction. These themes are too social, somehow, to describe the kind of deafness I want to identify. (Though it is true that Edna O'Brien, beautiful and sexy on the page as in life, really was chased out of town).

Hard to remember what it was like, back in 2013, but I seem to recall that you couldn't complain, in those days, without being told that other people had it worse. What women put up with was nothing compared to what happened to children in Catholic institutions. The wound can't be about gender, when Northern Ireland still bleeds. How can you harp on about the lyric voice, when women have no rights over their pregnant bodies? It was a pain competition, one that women could not win.

There is a difference between a culture that tilts male and a culture that does not see what it is doing; you might include the *London Review of Books* in the first category: only 25 per cent of books reviewed there in 2016 were by women. The arguments in the first tend to be about excellence, confidence, the prioritising of fact: it is possible that women are held to a different standard, but at least the arguments happen. In a culture that is unwittingly male, the tendency (I have found) is to take offence at the statistics. Awareness is itself problematic, so before you talk about inclusion you have to look at this aversion – a murky zone, where people are not entirely aware of themselves or of what they are pushing away.

Iris Murdoch famously said that being a woman 'is like being Irish … Everyone says you're important and nice, but you take second place all the time.'

I have spent most of my published life on predominantly male fiction lists based in the UK. The best of them are great and humane company on the page, but there is a confusion at the knotty end between great truths and ones that are merely horrible. This results in books charged by male anger, male violence and male self-disgust, sometimes expressed as misogyny. Successful male writers of Irish fiction are seldom 'manly' in this way. Their voices are often restrained, gentle or lyrical, with a distinctive number of books taking a female or a child's point of view. There is also a modernist strand of Irish fiction in which language is chaotically disturbed and remade. I might mention our tragic muse. Sometimes it seems as though Irish fiction of the last few decades is unusually powerless: you get books in which syntax refuses to cohere, novels in which a sense of agency is punished, or fails to matter. These novelists might be said to write 'like' women. They are rarely misogynistic, and this makes the whole difficulty harder to see. Fiction, as a trade, is fraught by the thrills and anxieties of feminisation. When a woman writes 'like' woman this tension disappears. There is also, weirdly, an added sense of authority. Irish men writing about women are sometimes praised for their insight, as though this was something women were incapable of saying for themselves.

The country where I grew up in the 70s was insular and impoverished, and the idea of greatness was very important to us. Books were not just an escape from the present, difficult moment, their greatness was a talisman against shame. The fact that *Ulysses*, the greatest of them all, also glories in the transgressive and the filthy, kept the ironies in motion. In order to become properly iconised, as he was on that old 'Irish Writers' poster, it was important that Joyce be dead.

An awareness of the writer's gravesite, the impulse to build statues and monuments, all of this was useful when it came to the national work of building a better past for ourselves. The deadness of the writer is especially interesting because they feel so alive on the page: this makes their books a talisman not just against shame but also against mortality. And this makes me wonder – and I have no answer to this – whether women will ever feel dead in the same way.

Many people have looked at the original 'Irish Writers' poster, that trite but effective iteration of the canon, and wondered, to take one example, why Brendan Behan should be preferred over Elizabeth Bowen. Maybe she just wouldn't look right on a pub wall. Bowen seems to be, not just the wrong gender, but also the wrong class, the wrong religion. This sense of wrongness does not adhere to Synge, Beckett, Swift, Goldsmith, O'Casey, Yeats, G. B. Shaw, or Wilde, who were all Protestant. There are three Catholics, Joyce, Flann O'Brien and Kavanagh, but none of these men, apart from Kavanagh, came from the farming background so beloved of Irish nationalism. The strong representation of playwrights on the poster is a reflection, perhaps, of the role of the theatre in forming ideas of a nation. In the years after Irish independence, women were slowly exiled, not just from the public house, but also from the playhouse, so the discussion about the canon has to include questions about public storytelling as well as ones about colonialism, or the middle class.

An equivalent poster about English or British writers would lean towards the nineteenth century, and would not be complete without Austen, Emily Brontë or George Eliot. The few novelists on the Irish version, wrote, in a way that neither Austen nor Bowen ever could, not just about the poor and the marginal, but transgressively about backsides and excrement (Joyce is the only one who wrote about sex). I looked at these writers pondering ideas of noble rot, and I remembered instead their childish glee.

Drinking is another kind of transgression, and the connection between drinking culture and writing culture remains a lucrative one today. Who takes their ideas of literary importance from a pub wall? The Irish tourist industry, certainly, along with their key market in the Irish diaspora. The tilt towards the male gets even steeper in America, with its emigrant nostalgia for an Irish past.

Shaw once said that 'Silence is the most perfect expression of scorn', but silence is the most perfect expression of anything at all, and this is the smart thing about exclusion, it is hard to call out, or identify. The real problem with silence, is that it is also silencing. People are, by exclusion, slowly undone.

Once you get inside the sense of circumference that a tradition provides, the issue becomes not one of acceptance but of status; hierarchies are made and remade, and the writers anxiety about critical authority becomes more problematic. What is the difference between authority and dominance? The game of top dog is not something I understood until I got an actual dog, when I realised that dominance requires submission. For women, this sometimes contains a troubling, erotic content, but it is not, strictly speaking, a gendered thing. Men snarl at each other too (and younger men pink up, sometimes, in adoration).

Which makes me wonder if Irish men have been the victims, not just of the feminising insult that is colonialism, now long past, but of other wounded hierarchies: damaged fathers, rotten priests, corrupt or weak political authority. As we shift away from the damage, the question about nationalism refuses to go away. What happens when men believe something together, or try to believe it? What do they have to expel in order to stake territory, claim a history and form a shared identity. It amazes me that the men who spend their time explaining Ireland, seldom pause to explain the persistent recurrence of bias in our cultural life.

As the woman's placard on the Trump march said: 'I can't believe I still have to protest this fucking shit'. Though I never did protest it, much, I just got on with writing books, as did other Irish women writers over the last 30 years. Much of this work was welcomed in the newspapers, though the language used can feel a little dated, now, and sometimes sought to reassure. It was just hard, given the general climate, to feel a sense of momentum.

It's not hard now. Whatever is happening feels like it is happening all the time. In the last six years there has been a constant stream of notable debuts by Irish women, to complement the constant stream of notable debuts by Irish men. These women are not shy and unassuming (unless they are), nor are they screaming through the air, lunatic (unless they want to be). They are publishing in a time of cultural shift, and into a new awareness, one that is fed by social media, acknowledged in print, supported by publishers and encouraged by festival curators. At least I hope they are. I hope we will finally sit side by side – in the newspapers, on the stage, up on the damn poster – men and women together.

If there is one thing I have come to believe over 30 years of writing fiction, if there is one sentence I would like to leave with you, as a legacy of my Laureateship, it is this: There is plenty of room.

OH CANADA

LECTURE DELIVERED ON THE PRESENTATION OF THE UCD ULYSSES MEDAL TO MARGARET ATWOOD

6 JUNE 2018

I was always the youngest in my class. At 16 I was considered too young for university, so in the spring before my final exams, I looked to fill a gap year as an au pair. I think it was my German teacher who pointed out an ad in the back of the newspaper for the United World Colleges instead – a strange looking school that seemed blessedly free of babies to mind. My mother, hardwired to the word 'scholarship', signed the application form, not realising I would, six months later, be packing a bag. I got the place, and, in September of 1979, I looked out of the window on the Rocky Mountains below. For the next two years I studied (not very hard) in an international school in the forests of Vancouver Island together with 200 students from 52 different countries. When I arrived, I asked when there was hot water available for showers and the Canadians laughed. What a question. There was always hot water. Where was I from, 1953?

In my first English class, the teacher, Theo Dombrowski, handed out a sheet with three poems to discuss: the first was a winsome, tough little poem by E. E. Cummings, called *My Sweet Old Etcetera*.

My sweet old etcetera
Aunt Lucy during the last war,
could and what's more
did tell you what everyone was fighting for

The second was a poem I already knew by Keats, *La Belle Dame Sans Merci*, which is about death, more or less, in the form of a beautiful woman (not, I suspect, the way that death will come to me). It contains the line 'She looked at me as she did love, and made sweet moan'.

'Well,' said Theo. 'We all know what that means.'

Well, I thought, we all certainly didn't, not until you pointed it out to us. After class I approached him. I took him to task for ruining the poem, which was a high and beautiful object, and one that I held dear. I was really quite cross. I accused him, pretty much, of having a filthy mind. I was 16. Theo Dombrowski was then 36. We have been friends ever since.

Theo grew up in Port Alberni, a logging town on Vancouver Island pervaded by the stink of the sawmill, not unlike the high note in the Liffey, back in the days of the Clondalkin Paper Mills. In this small town he fell in love with his wife Eileen, learned to play that fine Polish instrument the box accordion, taught himself piano, listened to opera, tried his hand as an artist, and got himself into University of British Columbia, where he wrote his doctoral thesis on *Ulysses* by James Joyce. Not many Joyceans jogged in 1979, but Theo jogged, swam, lumberjacked, taught Ukrainian dancing. Theo could do anything – including the rude bits of Keats. He loved a good fight. There was a major barney over the tundish scene in *The Portrait of the Artist as a Young Man* that got a bit physical. Cushions were sometimes thrown.

I was too busy quivering with disbelief, in that first class, to listen to the third poem, though a line of it stayed with me for many years after.

> Each time I hit a key
> on my electric typewriter,
> speaking of peaceful trees
> another village explodes

Five years later, when I turned 21, I got an electric typewriter as a present from my family. This was long before the pattering hush of the electronic keyboard – electric typewriters are pretty fierce objects, very mechanical, they are the gatling guns of the typing life. These remembered lines became set in the rhythms of my typing, and also in my terror of the blank page.

Each time I hit a key
on my electric typewriter,
another village explodes

I had lost the peaceful trees from the quotation, over time. A few years ago, I chased the reference in one of my letters to Theo, and he sent a copy of the poem back to me – chosen for the class, he said, because of its, 'wonderful sinister nervousness.' The poem is called *It is Dangerous to Read Newspapers* and it is by Margaret Atwood. In it, the poet is beset by images of violence, war and mass slaughter. It is hard to tell if this anxiety is for the self or for the victims. 'I am the cause' she says, though she is not the cause, or barely the cause, of a world in which corpses are bulldozed into pits. *It is Dangerous to Read Newspapers* owes something to the flayed sensibility of Plath, and it is stalled in the same kind of murderous passivity as *My Life Had Stood, a Loaded Gun* by Emily Dickinson, but the poem is also a challenge to the writer's neurotic distance from the world: how we thrive on pain – even the pain of others – without doing anything to fix it.

Atwood is Theo's favourite writer or – as he tactfully came to say after I started to publish – his 'other favourite writer'. Later that year he would give me *Surfacing* to read, Atwood's second novel in which a woman loses herself, both literally and metaphorically, in the forests of Northern Quebec.

Maybe he was just trying to get me out of the house. I was just 17 and I spent a lot of time smoking and having large thoughts about myself. *Surfacing* seemed like a guide to having your nervous breakdown out in the fresh air, of which there is no shortage in Canada. The school was always dragging you out into it. I would find myself stumbling along some or other trail, to see cougar tracks cross an empty beach, or to eat mussels as long as your hand, picked fresh from the rocks. At the end of the first of these hikes, still jet lagged – after ospreys and cormorants, no orcas, but maybe a sea otter (unless it was some kind of seal) – I staggered into a camping ground to find the driftwood already stacked, the bags of marshmallows heaped, the chord sequence of *Four Strong Winds* printed out on – possibly laminated – cards, and a line of portaloos in a clearing, standing guard. And behind the portaloos were hundreds of whispering miles of old-growth forest. And what did it whisper, the forest?

'Enjoy your marshmallows, guys. My goodness they look good.'

If you have ever been on the west coast of British Columbia you will remember the height of the Douglas Fir, the cool grey of Sitka Spruce, and the way their relentless verticality is broken by the arbutus, a broadleaf evergreen, with easy, curving branches and a red outer bark that flakes over inner bark that is cool, smooth and almost green. It is a little like our own Kerry Strawberry tree, a little like a tree they call, in Latin America, the Gringo because it peels red just like a white man's skin. This arbutus is the most touchable, most climbable tree you could imagine. And though I have seen the scrubby Irish version as far away as Australia, the magnificent Arbutus Menziesii does not travel much or well. It is difficult to propagate because, according to Theo, in order to germinate, the seed has to pass through the digestive tract of a particular bird. I think there are two specimens in Ireland, and they are both lonely. One of them is outside the canteen in RTE just a mile down the road from my office now in UCD. It is a relic of botanical tourism, undertaken in the nineteenth century, by the owners of Montrose House. And though, when in Canada, I stayed indoors smoking and talking while heartier students scaled mountains and rescued beached whales, I did, quietly and out of the corner of my eye, really love that tree. In my mid-20s I worked as a producer in RTE, and I left one or other meeting with management in Montrose House to walk over to the canteen, looking for a cup of coffee, or a place to cry, the tree was there for me, as a clear and growing representation of other realities, languages and possibilities.

At Christmas, the first year I was in Canada, I went to Winnipeg for deep cold, staying with a student's family in a kind of gingerbread house; a thing with wooden eaves and shutters, and triple glazing, there was more food, more baking, more cinnamon and egg nog, than I thought possible. It was a non-stop round of kindness, ease, bounty, cross-country skiing, patterned socks and positivity. I am still, you know, slightly suspicious of positivity, which means I am always a stranger in Canada, or in some parts of it.

Another Christmas was spent in a cabin with three other students on Galliano Island, in the Juan de Fuca Straight, my first sight of a forest landscape after fire, when we hiked in darkness over the spine of the island to fill our rucksacks with oysters, which we ate for three or four days after. I don't know why we hiked in the middle of the night. Perhaps, being teenagers, we just forgot the get up during the day. My recollection of those years is also the recollection of the enormous, wonderful epic sleeping I did in one place or another. I dreamt for hours. I dreamt in five acts. After Galliano, I went up to Powell River, to stay with Grace, a fellow student and a member of The Tla'ammon First Nation. Her family had a bow and arrow on the wall and a neighbour with a trash can full of emptied bottles of mouthwash, and they were delighted by my sleeping. They praised its epic duration. They let me sleep on, undisturbed by heartiness or egg nog, cinnamon buns, hayrides and fun.

That was the week it snowed in BC. And if you think Ireland panics in the snow then my goodness, you should chase yourself some weather down the western edge of Canada where no one has snow tires and one rare car slews into another rare car on the forest roads on the one day it comes down, not because the surface is slippy but because the drivers are gone pure hysterical.

At the end of my two years as a student in Canada, I hitch-hiked from Victoria to Calgary with two female friends. We went over the Rockies, to get our fill of bears: brown bears at the dumpsters, and up on a ridge, on the day we crossed the continental divide, the standing shape of a grizzly. Or is that my organising brain? To put a bear that is known for the ridge on its neck, in the place where the planet itself gathers up into a ridge that runs the length of North America? I don't know. I do remember the bear, humpy and vertical, and far away, as we stuck our thumbs out more desperately for a lift from one or other crazy guy in a pickup truck. The guys in the pickups were, without a single exception, crazy. And they kept us, sometimes a little obsessively, safe from the other drivers, who they said were *really* crazy.

Before we set off on that trip, we stopped in Victoria to browse at a bookshop which, I realised a few years later, was the same shop that appeared in stories of a Canadian writer I had discovered called Alice Munro. For reading material on that trip I bought *The Edible Woman* by Margaret Atwood which contained an amount of thinking about food. This I read on the camping tables of Banff and the Okanagan Valley where I ate asparagus for the first time – we just bought from a farmer on the side of the road and boiled up on a gas stove. I turned the pages of *The Edible Woman* both during and after my first experience of asparagus, and long before I realised that food itself could be a problem for some people. It was also the first time, I think, that I read a book of fiction which contained questions about being a woman that were as much essential as political. It would be many years before I would describe myself as female in any interesting or serious way.

It does not seem like a lot to ask – that a novel should give you something to think about; that it might bring you a little further on. Bringing us all a bit further on is a habit of Atwood's, though sometimes we have to double back in order to find it. This is what the world recently discovered, revisiting *The Handmaid's Tale*, a book I thought charming when I read it in 1985, and not entirely untrue.

Meanwhile, back in 1981, *The Edible Woman* was The Thing I brought home from Canada, it went into my luggage for the flight home, another epic sleeping event, which involved an engine failing or dropping off (which surely could not be possible), and me waking up on the tarmac, expecting Amsterdam and finding Edmonton.

Because I was there so young, and it was so far away, Canada still seems to be a place separated from my adult life both by geography and by time. It is hard for me to make connections between it and my life now. I did not think it possible, for example, that Esi Edugyan could live in Colwood, which was the place I used to go to buy shampoo when I was 17. How could a writer live *there*? Returning to Victoria for a writer's festival, someone points out the house where Carol Shields used to live. This is on the way to the house of James Munro, the man who ran that bookshop with Alice, and I really don't believe this can be real. Here I am – impossibly! – back in the stories I read 30 years ago; stories I read in order to be reminded of this town. Or I am back in Alice Munro's life before she wrote those stories, or in my own life before I read them when, for two dreaming years, I lived just down the road. Another time, in Toronto, crossing the Bloor St Viaduct, the site of Ondaatje's first chapter from *In the Skin of a Lion*, finds me banging on the window of the mini-van, the way Theo Dombrowski, from Port Alberni, might give an involuntary yelp, in Dublin, at the sight of the James Joyce Tower.

People have a thing about Ireland, they pull all kinds of significance out of a landscape, which is, let's face it, pretty tame stuff – a few green bumps, an amount of rain. Canada does something similar for me. In Newfoundland, I talk to Lisa Moore on a ferry that sails from Farewell to Fogo Island, and I don't know if it is Lisa, or her work, or the extreme remoteness of the spot, but I realise that a mood of many years is lifting, just then. Something has happened. Some change.

ENNIS, ARMAGH, HOWTH AND BALLYMUN

Last year, a student writer told me that novelists are not supposed to use lists; 'but you do it all the time.' She seemed a little cross. I didn't know who was telling her what she was supposed to do, apart from some finger-wagging inner voice – that same voice it was my mission, as a teacher, to unmask. But she had a point. Yes, they can be overdone. And, guilty as charged: I am prone to a list. I blame *Faith Healer* by Brian Friel. I blame Ireland, because the easiest list to fall into is one of Irish towns. In fact, you have to be careful with the name of even a single Irish town, it so easily becomes a sentimental thing. These names do a lot of work on the page: put them in a list and they turn epic, lyrical, sad. Before you know, you will be singing it.

As Laureate for Irish Fiction my duties involved teaching students at UCD and NYU, writing lectures, curating an annual event and, one way or another, visiting a number of Irish towns. It is all in the way you arrange them. So, Cavan, Navan, Cork and Ballyshannon sounds like a children's rhyme, which is not the tone we are looking for here (we will leave that to, P. J. Lynch who is Laureate na nÓg). Let me try for a more adult syncopation: Belfast, Limerick, Galway, Cavan, Ennis, Armagh, Howth and Ballymun. Kells and Carlow, Bantry, Ballyshannon, Dublin, Longford, and Listowel. Sligo, Tallaght, Wexford, Cork. Stradbally, Navan, Carrick-on-Shannon, Dromineer and Tullamore.

Some of these were official events, delivering lectures or meeting readers groups as part of a series called 'The Reader's Voice' which was done with the *Sean O'Rourke Show* on RTE. There were also short story events

– because everyone loves a short story and no one, unfortunately, buys them. Others again were part of a resolution I made to accept invitations in Ireland, if I could. Added to which were a good number of book launches or celebratory events in Dublin, the occasional embassy (I seem to have given up white wine) and events in America, at NYU, the Irish Arts Centre, Princeton, and for PEN International. There were 1916 commemoration events on both sides of the pond. I did not find it exhausting. I was the Laureate: I knew what I was for.

Hard to believe when you read some of the things they produce, but writers are often shy. Readers, especially Irish ones, are also often shy. We meet in the shared privacy of the page and sometimes need the protection of a public voice. I realised I would not get through the Laureateship if I had to write speeches, so my new discipline was to sit on some form of public transport with my eyes closed and to arrive in front of a literary gathering ready to be mildly amusing or properly angry, because the right words, if you can find them, give people a sense of common purpose: they buoy up the lonely, which is all of us, and affirm the whole endeavour of writing books.

The writers hosted by the Laureateship makes another fine list: how about Kevin Barry, Claire Louise Bennett, Mary Costello and Colin Barrett, who read in Galway with music by Feargal Murray Camille O Sullivan. Or Tóibín, McInerney, McLoughlin, and McCormack in Dublin with music by Lisa O'Neill. And, on the radio, MacLaverty, McCloskey, Ryan, Dwyer-Hickey, Kilroy, Doyle. The last event was in Carlow Visual, with stories by Sally Rooney, Belinda McKeon, Colin Wash and Nicole Flattery, with music by Little John Nee.

I was appointed Laureate by the Arts Council in January 2015. The first official event took place in Longford Public Library, run by the mighty talent of librarian Mary Reynolds. I had plans to support Irish writing in translation and to promote the short story, but in fact what I ended up doing in the three years that followed was all, somehow, already present in that room. The people who had come to meet the new Laureate were readers, by which I mean they were the silent engine of the Irish tradition, energetic consumers of fiction with strong views that were seldom sought. They were also library users and, at a guess, people who listened to the radio. They included the parents of local writer Belinda McKeon, and also Louise Lovett who runs a women's centre in Longford. When I came back home, I realised it was 30 years to the day since her sister, Ann Lovett, had died in Granard.

I did not think I was appointed Laureate because I was a woman. The business of writing is hard enough without taking on the additional burden of gender politics. Listening to arguments about gender makes men mildly defensive and takes very little of their time. If you are a woman, making these arguments will eat your head, your talent and your life. None of this ever seemed to me fair, or even useful. But that gathering in Longford was telling me its own story. If it held the promise of books to come, it also held reminders of events that had shaped my own work, some of them unbearably sad. I am, by age and stage, a kind of bridge between a bright future for the voices of Irish women and a terrible past.

So, although I did not want to be partisan, the three lectures I wrote during the stint as Laureate were about the female voice, heard and unheard. For the first, in 2015, I had the privilege of meeting Catherine Corless for a piece about Antigone, the figure from Greek tragedy who called for the proper burial of the mute and dishonoured dead. The second was about the voice of *New Yorker* writer Maeve Brennan, long lost and now regained; and this was delivered in NYU near the streets where she used to walk. The third was about gender representation in the canon and in the review pages of the newspapers, including the

Irish Times. Ironically, for a piece about unheard voices, there was no echo or indication that it had been heard, but sometimes you just have to speak anyway.

As the inaugural Laureate I tried to balance a sense of civic engagement with the needs of my own work and failed. Hard to call it absolutely, but I would say that publication of my next novel was set back by a year. The Laureate is, first of all, a writer, but no two writers are the same, and each will have their own approach to the role. I need to meet readers, I find teaching very useful to my own work (no more lists!) and I am blocked, at the desk, by the feeling of things that are obviously going too long unsaid.

So, I found it useful. I hope it was useful to others. I enjoyed my temporary elevation. Now that particular ladder is gone, as the man said, it is back to the foul rag and bone shop of the heart.

'Solstice' and 'The Hotel' were read at The Long Night of the Short Story in 2017 (Project Arts Centre, Dublin) and 2018 (Visual, Carlow), and subsequently published in the *New Yorker*.

'Antigone in Galway' and 'Call me George' were first published in the *London Review of Books*. 'Maeve Brennan: Going Mad in New York' was published by the *Stinging Fly* as an Introduction to Brennan's 'The Springs of Affection' and extracted in the *Guardian*. 'Ennis, Armagh, Howth and Ballymun', was published in the *Irish Times* under the heading, 'Making Arguments about Gender Will Eat Your Head'.

Special thanks to Sarah Bannan, Literature Officer of the Arts Council of Ireland, and to Jen Coppinger, producer and manager of the Laureateship programme.

Thanks also to Marcella Bannon, to Dr Ken Keating for his researched figures on gender representation, to Margaret Kelleher, Deborah Landau in NYU, James Ryan at UCD, Deborah Treisman of the *New Yorker*, the editors of the *Guardian*, Martin Doyle at the *Irish Times*, Cormac Kinsella and to Noelle Moran in UCD Press.